Muddy Mysticism

The Sacred Tethers of Body, Earth, and Everyday

NATALIE BRYANT RIZZIERI

WOMANCRAFT PUBLISHING

Published by Womancraft Publishing, 2021
www.womancraftpublishing.com

ISBN 978-1-910559-65-9
Muddy Mysticism is also available in ebook format: ISBN 978-1-910559-64-2

Cover design, interior design and typesetting: Patrick Treacy, lucentword.com
Cover image © Tara Turner
Woodcut prints: Jef Thompson/Shutterstock.com

Womancraft Publishing is committed to sharing powerful new women's voices, through a collaborative publishing process. We are proud to midwife this work, however the story, the experiences and the words are the authors' alone. A percentage of Womancraft Publishing profits are invested back into the environment reforesting the tropics (via TreeSisters) and forward into the community.

Praise for Muddy Mysticism

With breath-taking lyricism, Natalie Bryant Rizzieri captures a new definition of the divine – one that shows us darkness can be holy, the prosaic a place of Mystery, and that the sacred can bleed in through the cracks. This searing provocation to reclaim what is sacred in our daily lives is tenderly excavated from the ruins of patriarchy and indoctrination. It is a brilliant debut: exquisitely crafted and an indelible classic.

Katherine Larson, author of *Radial Symmetry* and winner of the Yale Series of Younger Poets

Muddy Mysticism is a treasure-trove of wisdom for those who yearn for the mystic, but not by way of the cloister. It reveals a path that seeks spiritual presence amidst the ruckus and noise of everyday life, the struggles with children and partners, work and disappointment, loss and sorrow, through Natalie Bryant Rizzieri's blazingly honest telling of her own messy, holy process. It's not easy to be a poet and a mystic, with very young children, one still nursing at the book's beginning. For Rizzieri this difficulty is an opening into the healing mud of embodiment. Muddy Mysticism overturns conventional religious ideas that demonize desire, appetite, women's bodies, and the dark. Full of visionary gems, it offers a radical reorientation to the relationship between Body and Soul. In Rizzieri's company we are moved and inspired by the Mystery as it "leaks into" her own embodied experience with crying babies, spilt milk and the small miracles of amazement our children bring us every day. Accompany her on this profound path. She'll open the door leading out of the Patriarchy; she'll show you the Way to know the Real as Gift and Blessing.

Naomi Ruth Lowinsky, author of *The Motherline, The Sister from Below,* and *The Faust Woman Poems*

Contents

dedication

for the loosed and frayed and over-wintered,
for the wanderer and the searcher and the lonely,
for the empty, for the barefoot, and mostly for the voiceless,
for the one who screams no, for the one who whispers yes,
for the one who doesn't belong, and for the one on the edge,
for the sleepless, for the outcast, for the fighter, and for the rebel,
for the earthbound, for the homebound, for the burning,
for the weary and bedraggled, for the hungry, for the cold,
for the ordinary, and for the reformer,
for the one who wakes early and the one who stays up
all night for the very same reason,
for the one haunted with longing, for the disillusioned,
for the heretic who is also a dreamer, yes, for the dreamer,
for the one who wants to know God more
than has ever seemed possible,
and for the one who no longer wants to try,
for the one who doesn't know how to define the divine,
for the one who doesn't even attempt to,
for the one who doesn't know where to begin,
for the one for whom it never ends,
for the one who has never reached the horizon,
for the one who never even reaches,
for the one who sits under elevated train tracks,
for the one who misses the stars,
for the skeptic.

It is for you I write.

The work of the world is common as mud.

— Marge Piercy [1]

Maybe the soul is only a still place
in the body,
The eye and not the eye,
Something both like an altar
And like a sill opening onto a distant landscape.

— Larry Levis [2]

Foreword

by Elizabeth Robinson

What if to be a mystic is to be pregnant? What if mysticism is a form of gestation? Like pregnancy, mystical experience involves the recognition of a greater – an *other* – presence with whom the seeker unites in the deepest intimacy. In pregnancy, one wonders: is this thing I'm gestating going to overtake me? Where do "I" end and "it" begins? In pregnancy, as with mystical experience, a woman lives with an uneasily divided subjectivity and we live with the body's "prophetic imagination." Who is the center and where is the periphery? Mysticism disrupts our conventional sense of agency as the mystic wonders who it is speaking. Is it the self or the Presence? Each nurtures the other and thus the boundaries of the self evanesce into a halo of energy and light.

But as glorious as pregnancy is, it is also profoundly disruptive. It can make us queasy. It disorients. It changes our center of gravity. It makes us crave strange, possibly inappropriate, things. It exhausts. We cannot control the changes that it sets in motion. And at its fulfillment? We open to birth in pain. Blissful motherhood? Transcendent love? No, birth happens by the rule of the body: bloody, sweaty, grunting to emit a being who is part of the self whom the self has never before met. By the time the baby is born, when the real work of nurture begins, the mother wonders at the commitment she has made. She is to mother a being whose life extends beyond hers: it is her quest to make child or Presence free for its own agency and creation. Yet now, she simply longs for a shower, a sip of water, a rest. The journey has just begun.

In *Muddy Mysticism*, Natalie Bryant Rizzieri takes us on this journey. Having literally birthed three babies, she essays the birth of her mystic self and it is messy, subversive, and sometimes anguishing. Bryant Rizzieri claims the pain and confusion of this birthing as her rite and right as a mystic, asserting, "I am uncoupling mysticism from the denial of the flesh." Her claim is for a mode of transcendence that is anti-transcendent. Her mysticism is embodied. Her mysticism stealthily woos the quotidian. There, mystery is held in capably large hands and freckled arms.

Against Bryant Rizzieri's vision lies the long history of patriarchal theology. After all, doesn't the divine issue forth from the clouds, from some version of "out there"? In my younger son's toddlerhood, he patiently explained to me that God is an old man with a long white beard who lives in the sky. Appalled, I asked him where he had heard this. Assessing my alarm, he shrugged, "Well, actually no. God is the sun." The divine, even in a three year old's estimation, was safely aloft and, of course (of course!) definitively male.

Muddy Mysticism doesn't just resist this tradition, Bryant Rizzieri (through apparently vast study) finds again for us the vestiges of a mystical history that glories in the immanent. As though that weren't enough, she brings her lived experience as lover, mother, and activist to life. Hearing her account of the baby at her breast, I could not resist wondering if the mystic could be found in the figure of a nursing mother. Here's an unexpected inversion! In a grounded, immanent, domestic mysticism, Reality nestles at one's very breast and the mystic feeds that warm and pulsing presence with her sweet milk. Is the mystic the haven for the mystery? Yes, she holds it in her arms. It is the nursing mother who knows, as her breasts fill in a rush, that her child is about to wake and turn to her. These processes are more than biology: they are uncanny, prescient. They reveal the workings of the unseen world that we are taught to, and strive to, ignore. The breast that leaks milk at the cry of the child has awareness beyond our casual daily pragmatism.

So much for the sky gods of yore. Yet Bryant Rizzieri's examination doesn't merely conclude with a dismantling of divine hierarchies, she also pushes hard against our stereotype of the mystic as an isolated hermit:

I had to attempt to find the divine in the immanent, in the pleasure of my children's hands in mine, in the earthbound, in the the sounds of a crying toddler. I had to learn to transform what I had assumed was interference into a sacred way – seeing these perceived obstacles as entrances.

This mysticism is not singular. It is, in ways that we barely understand, communal. What a relief to see it affirmed that Presence lives so richly in the familial, in conversations with friends, in poems shared. Holiness abounds in dirty laundry, the tangle of toys on the floor, a sleepless, teething baby. Holiness with holes – not that imaginary stream of perfection in which, we assume, the enlightened can float. Sometimes the sacred has a clumsy gravity. Sometimes, the mystical is negotiated and painful. We make much in Western tradition of the metaphor of weddedness to a divine spouse. Those who live the reality of marriage day by day know that, mixed with eros and intimacy, understanding and assurance, married life can be confusing, maddening, exhausting and lonely. A profoundly important message issues from *Muddy Mysticism*. Our sacredness is not ours to own, but rather ours to cultivate, even argue over, and to share.

Our bodies are complex systems in which our spirits dwell, but they never dwell alone. As Bryant Rizzieri notes, the unborn child leaves his or her cells in the maternal body. In that great gestation, we commingle with so many presences, a community of cells, a legacy of souls. We depart and return to each other. The wholeness of the mystery, as we begin to gather it, ferments in birth, but also in death. My first son was born as his grandfather was dying, and I felt certain that they met in transit, passing in different directions through the same portal. Bryant Rizzieri hallows this paradox when her baby is born in the same season that her sister's baby dies. She writes, "Death and birth are horribly and gorgeously intertwined. They are intimates; they are borderlands. And the feeling in both [...] places is that of longing – sacred and ordinary both." Yes, the irreconcilable lives in mysticism too. We remain part of a larger wholeness even when grief

makes us unable to understand or comfort each other. The sacred is
conceived from desire, but there is no true follower who would deny
Presence can be born, and borne, out of unappeased questioning and
loss.

Natalie Bryant Rizzieri wrestles with all of this. For much of this
book, she makes a home for her children, seeks homes for vulnerable
people who lack them, but cannot call herself "at home" in the place
where she lives. Her account intimates that the mystic lives in vari-
ous forms of exile. Even moving to the place that one wants to call
home can be wrenching. Through her honesty, we come to understand
that the holy is a quixotic, irresistible call to something that even the
most ardent believer sometimes doubts. Those of us who are so blessed
with doubt paradoxically continue to believe with our entire souls and
bodies.

Welcome to this cranky, necessary, beautiful blessing. It abides
in the limits of the body that craves sleep, food, and uninterrupted
thought. Its still small voice resonates among children with runny
noses and greasy cowlicks. Muddy mysticism anoints the finitude of
human life by recognizing that something extraordinary arises from
deficit, if we permit it to do so. Perhaps mysticism is really a study of
– a venturing into – paucity, rupture, uncertainty: an embrace of the
wrongness of the world. Here is an embrace so tenacious that, should
we accept its challenge, detritus overflows into fullness. Amid the
brokenness, we discover that "the center of mysticism is belovedness"
where we've finally found our home and it is very, very good.

Introduction

River inside the river.
World within the world.
All we have is words
To reveal the rose
that the rose obscures.

— Gregory Orr[3]

Although it wasn't initially obvious to me, skepticism is the implicit posture of this book – deep skepticism about the presence of the divine in our daily lives. Whenever it seems otherwise, or maybe especially when it seems otherwise, do not be deceived. This book is my response to my own frequent despair that things are not okay. This is my wondering aloud if the divine is ever found in places that seem unlikely to someone steeped in Western dualism and raised in the Christian tradition – especially in my own prosaic life. This is the book I had to write in order not to lose track of the divine. These musings were my way to survive the "disappearance" of God and were my stepping stones to a more pervasive understanding of the Mystery.

One summer day, deep in the heart of Queens and in the throes of mothering two young children, I began rummaging through my books on spirituality. I have long been enchanted by the mystics – Hafiz, Teresa of Avila, Rumi, St. John of the Cross, Adelia Prado, and Hildegard von Bingen, to name a few. Even since stumbling away from organized religion and a very conservative strand of evangelical Christianity, I remain drawn to the mystics because of their deep and abiding hunger to experience the divine. I relate to that hunger. I am driven by it. And I know I am not alone. So many of us who were raised in evangelical Christianity, who were schooled in morality over mysticism, who were taught to trust in scriptures over trust in oneself, who were offered private salvation over collective action and justice, and taught to value doctrine over direct experience, have been left empty-handed and hungry. Many of us have gone searching for a new and even mystical way – one that would not only cease to ostracize the sublunary and denigrate daily life but would also elevate it – along with its nuances, sensuality, ashes, darkness, uncertainty, and silence. Many of us seek a mysticism of belonging as differentiated from inclusivity, which unfortunately still implies that there is an "in" and an "out".

In my search, and despite a handful of interruptions from a crying toddler who was lying outside my door, I looked through my books, many of which chronicle various mystical and spiritual paths, hoping to find proof that it was possible to maintain a substantial spiritual practice while mothering small children and living in the largest city in the United States. Both were a stretch for me, being an introvert accustomed to spending most of my days alone and as a forest dweller living in New York City for the sake of my husband. I was struggling against the lack of wild and calm spaces within and without.

After leaving organized religion, I had to relearn how to connect with the Mystery. I wanted to know the truth of Jack Spicer's words in "After Lorca" when he said, "As things decay, they bring their equivalents into being," but I was not yet convinced. I needed the equivalent (and maybe even the opposite) of an old, religious, belief-oriented, transcendent connection within a new framework, within a new body, even, and within a new context. I knew how to connect with Mystery in pristine wilderness, in solitude, in beauty, as a hermit, and within organized religion. But none of these avenues were available to me any longer. Could I be so blessed that in the necessity of relinquishing these cherished ways, I could make something new and real?

This day I was feeling particularly desperate. With two children, the tangles of a large city, a marriage, and a job running a non-profit I founded to support abandoned individuals with special needs in Armenia, there was no denying that I was held fast and tethered to the earth by my own gravity, the weight of my family and those I served and loved. This was not at all how I imagined mystics to be. I had bought into and internalized the historical myth that was reiterated time and again that women's work was less valuable. In *Wild Mercy: Living the Fierce and Tender Wisdom of the Female Mystics*, Mirabai Starr says that "Every culture and religious tradition controlled by men has placed higher importance on scriptural study and ritual observance than on feeding babies and cleaning up after them. Women have internalized our own devaluation." I had done the same. This was not the context in which I had sustained a mystical practice for the years prior. An annual week or two of solitude and study had disappeared entirely with nursing and raising babies. The wilderness was unreachable due to traffic and suburb after suburb. Rituals that I had carefully crafted when childless were impossible with the near constant interruptions. Beauty had to be completely redefined and reclaimed.

A few nights before, we had a family over for dinner that my husband, Aaron, had recently met at the park. Jude, my eldest, didn't like having new people in our home. He wasn't apt to curb his thoughts for the sake of decorum. I could see his frustration building as the nine of us sat crammed around a small table made for six. Finally, he turned to me, his face red as a coral bead, and said, "I want to take this glass and break it and use the glass to cut these people." I'll say it again: my life was not what I imagined a mystic's life to be.

So, I dug through books and memories, stories and conversations. To my further despair, I came up all but empty handed. In one anthology of notable individuals within the Christian tradition, only three women out of hundreds were even included. Three. Not one of them was a person of color, even though people of color were the original Christian mystics. Not one of them was married or had children. Even in more recent books that weave together mystical voices of women, in particular, and explore divine feminine symbols from various traditions, the examples given are women who were pilgrims and were not mothers or caregivers. Granted, women did not have much choice on either front given their historical context, but that is entirely the problem. At many times during history, it would have been too risky for women to speak out, to gather openly, and to claim her own spiritual authority. As a result, white men in societies that only rarely included women, and especially women with children, have written most of the mystical texts we read today.

I needed a more earthbound and feminist exploration of mysticism written for those of us who have chosen willingly and purposefully to abide primarily in the temporal world, written by a woman with children she desperately loves, written by a woman whose children say things like mine at the dinner table, written by someone surrounded by chaos and the unruly, written by someone who prioritized experience over the construct of belief, written by someone who didn't want to appropriate another culture's beloved traditions but who, nonetheless, needed something on which to hang their heart.

I know for certain that I am not the only individual with children filled with an insatiable longing to exist within the heart of the sacred. I see a deep and absorbing hunger in women and men alike to create a unique, fulfilling, and even mystical spiritual path outside of the bounds of organized religion. I hear about it on the playground. I see it in my book club. And most of us don't want to become hermits (at least not on a typical day). We want to hold down jobs and possibly raise children. We don't want to be required to give up our identities as women or parents. We don't want to have to trade our identities in for this longing.

So, I wrote the book I most needed, within an experience of exile from the forest and from the God of my childhood. I wrote as a wife and mother, all of which seemed at first glance to disqualify me from the path of a mystic. I did not want the atypical mystical terrain of these years to be lost. And just as importantly, I did not want to lose the divine in this season of my life. And this was at risk, largely due to the fact that I didn't have anyone to show me the way and because my life no longer had the structure and space that had previously allowed me to experience the divine.

I had to start over.

I determined then and there to make a mystical path where others may have deemed that impossible and to chronicle my own prosaic (sometimes joyful, sometimes infuriating) existence as *that mystical path* toward the heart of the divine. I had already left behind the path of organized religion but had to furthermore decide that, at least for now, I must leave the path of transcendence behind as well. I had to attempt to find the divine in the immanent, in the pleasure of my children's hands in mine, in the earthbound, in the sounds of a crying toddler. I had to learn to transform what I had assumed was interference *into* a sacred way – seeing these perceived obstacles as entrances. What I did not know yet was that the question was not how to maintain a spiritual practice in this season but rather how mothering two small children in New York City could actually *be* my spiritual practice.

I invite you to do the same – to discover through these pages that the shape of your unique and muddy life can in fact be your mystical path. I dare to place these words into your hands and in my wildest prayers, hope that these words will spur you toward your own articulation – that you will create a mosaic with the beautiful and broken pieces of your life. As Alexander Chee says in his essay, *How to Unlearn Everything*, "Most of what has survived to us thus far is literature written by white male writers. The last three decades especially have seen a struggle to revive the books we have lost – books by women, people of color, and queer writers – and to then try and write out of that recuperation a new tradition." If you are a woman, I invite you to help me craft – through the dailiness of your own life – a robust feminist or archetypally feminine description of mysticism. If you are a man, I invite you to participate in an embodied feminine mysticism and to help craft a profoundly embodied masculine description of mysticism. If you are a person of color or a queer writer, I am searching for your unique (or possibly lost or appropriated) descriptions of mysticism. Let's reclaim mysticism from the confines of privilege and celebrate the immanent and earthbound. We will learn from one another, as these descriptions emerge through books, conversations, poems and music.

I am confident that there were mystics among those women and men, black and brown and white, who were exiled or oppressed, who prioritized family over education, rootedness over wandering, immanence over transcendence, experience over theology, dark over light, descent over ascent, and body over spirit. But we so rarely hear from them in this context and the voices that we do hear are diametrically opposed to the shape of my life, to motherhood, though not, as I would discover, necessarily to mysticism.

And even while I have no doubt that mystics have existed in each and every corner, category and confine, unchronicled mysticism does not serve those of us who are hungry for insight today or who may live in the periphery of the historical texts. Being a white woman, I can only help to remedy the dearth of public female voices who are in long-term intimate relationships, who have children and who live in the city. An archetypally feminine perspective of the divine is largely lost when we tell the story of history and it is our work to reclaim that through the fervor of articulation and practice. My only hope is that the very fact that a prosaic mysticism was left unwritten is an invitation to find our own particular way toward the heart of the divine. And one that will be always unfolding. To quote Alexander Chee again, we are "writing out of that recuperation a new tradition."[4] Our liberation is at stake, whether it be liberation from patriarchy, racism, oppression, dogma or an exclusively transcendent spiritual vision.

But what of the person who does not feel the presence of the sacred in their life in any way, shape or form and who longs for that experience? What of the person who has been so burned and betrayed by the systems that are built around the idea of the sacred that they do not want to come anywhere near? What of the person who is so weighed down by dogma or theology that she cannot even *experience*? This book is my effort at inviting people into a new way of being and seeing that is ever and always still unfolding for me – one that partakes of the divine with bones and breath. It is more akin to the householder's path in Buddhism, as opposed to the renunciate or monastic mentality. I did not grow up learning how to feel and see the sacred in this way – throughout the tapestry of my daily life. I was schooled instead in religious contexts and in cultivating transcendence. I was taught that God was light, and in Him was no darkness. But when I no longer found or felt God, when my life went dark and turned to midnight, I started looking for the Mystery in the muddy places, in the dirt beneath my feet, and some days even finding it. I definitely still do not always feel the sacred throughout my life, but I have learned that this inconsistency and variability haunts and stokes mystics within every tradition.

If truth be told, I think that it is desperation and hunger that enable me to occasionally experience life with a sense of the sacred as pervasive. By following longing, the flip side of desperation, there has been a slow shift in my perspective – simple openness to the moment as sacred, and a clinging to Pierre Teilhard de Chardin's claim that "Nothing here below is profane for those who know how to see."[5]

Chardin lived and wrote in the early 1900s. He was a French scientist and controversial Catholic philosopher and mystic who is known for his idea that humankind is evolving toward a final spiritual unity. And his ideas are particularly applicable here. If nothing is profane, then all is sacred. If all is sacred, then I am not locked out of experiencing the divine *no matter what.* If all is sacred, then it is just about seeing. And when it may not feel like I would expect the sacred to feel, I change my perception of the sacred to be wider still and to include something new, like the bathtub overflowing, and even sometimes, the vulnerabilities of my life – a death, a disagreement, trauma, discontent. These vulnerabilities may in fact be the primary portals to the divine, perhaps because they require surrender. And they will most definitely have a different texture for all of us.

For anyone who may be daunted, all I really mean by mystic is one who tries to be close to the real or to the ultimate reality, and one who seeks out direct experience with the sacred. While I don't take the validity of mysticism to be self-evident, I simply want to explore mysticism as a way of being, a kind of consciousness available to everyone in which we can explore "the art of union to the real." [6] But any book that dares to chronicle anything as numinous and shape-shifting as mysticism, will see it changing as soon as it is there on the page. Once it is written down, all the counterpoints will suddenly be noticeable all around. Add to this the long tradition of mystics contradicting themselves time and again often unabashedly and I hope I am in good company.

The truth is – I don't really know (or need to know) who or what or if God is. I have no comfortable or sole category of spiritual identity in which to place myself (and assuage some of you, dear readers). I have multiple ways that I claim as my own and my life is rich and complicated because of it. Despite my lack of affiliation, I still see religion as a container for the sacred, just not a necessary one.

I believe along with Wallace Stevens that "it can never be satisfied, the mind, never" especially when it comes to God. And to try to name something that the mind cannot comprehend is a challenge in and of itself. In this spirit, I hold the names and ideas of God I have chosen to use in these pages with open hands. Some of them have flown away since the writing of this book. Some of them have stayed with me.

Some nights, I try spoken prayers with my son, Jude. I asked him last night which name of God he wanted me to use. He immediately said, "Sophia." We used to pray to Mother God or Father God, but not lately. Sophia speaks to him right now – wisdom personified. This particular face and name of the Mystery touches him. The fact that we can call on God by many names does not threaten or divide God, but gathers the Mystery from all corners of earth, soul, body, sea. When Jude woke this morning, he asked what name of God his best friend uses. I told him I do not know. Nor do I need to. And she might not use one at all.

But all I really mean and cannot mean by God is the ultimate reality, which undergirds the universe and in which we all abide and in us also abides. I mean the same thing by divine, sacred, God, Mystery, and Real and use these terms interchangeably. The poet Daniel Ladinsky said it well when he said: "What can entwine all this in its arms? What a / container there must be that some, still hung up on names, call...God."[7] Names and symbols of the divine are inadequate to speak of the Real and quickly lose their meaning, sometimes just as soon as I scratch them onto the page. But I do not yet know of any other way to speak.

Just as it is complicated to speak of God, it is equally complicated to wade into the waters of gender, racism and social constructs, but I inevitably do because to pretend to avoid these concepts and constructs is something only a person of privilege can do. While I am a white woman and while I do believe we need female voices to speak of mysticism, offering a counterpoint and balance to the available mystical body of literature, I also want to be careful not to create or describe an exclusive female or feminine way of being. Additionally, although I identify as a female, I am not exclusively feminine myself and as far as I understand it, we all contain the feminine and the masculine in varying degrees. I think of Rebecca Solnit's words in her memoir:

The names of the colors are sometimes cages containing what doesn't belong there, and this is often true of language generally, of the words like woman, man, child, adult, safe, strong, free, true, black, white, rich, poor. We need the words, but use them best knowing they are containers forever spilling over and breaking open. Something is always beyond.[8]

That said, in these pages, I am unabashedly seeking a more feminine face of God – because the realm of this book is in the muddy places and there is historically and archetypally a more natural affinity between the earthy and feminine faces of God. But when speaking of the feminine, I am referring primarily to the archetypal feminine – feral and subversive qualities as well as tenderness, compassion, mercy and unknowing. The feminine does not see with a harsh and glaring light. It sees from all sides. It is a circling. I realize that even the archetypal associations are laden and sometimes overburdened with problematic social, cultural and political connotations. But even so, I believe that there is clarity to be gained around this immense topic of mysticism and its links to the feminine.

One of the first people I read who attempts to define and describe a mystical feminist theology was Beverly Lanzetta. She is a theologian who also writes about the concept of global spirituality and new monasticism. In her life-changing book *Radical Wisdom*, she says:

There comes a point in a woman's spiritual life when she is in uncharted territory... She must forge her own path, because even her religious traditions fail her. Certainly, there have always been heroic women who stalked the wild rocky shores of women's authentic self – and who risked the perilous journey of returning to the bunker of women's daily existence. But only a few women have left traces of their search for a feminist God, a God who is radical and intimate enough to be on the side of women's divine humanity.

This book is my trace of a search for a feminist God and I hope it leads you to leave your own trace as well. This is my search for an awareness that the divine lives in the streets, in the throes of family life, in my particular day-to-day. This is my articulation of a sublunary and muddy mysticism that is equally available to men and women alike but remains intertwined and earthy, sense-oriented and variable, and interdependent with all beings and all things.

I want to clarify right away that a feminine-oriented mysticism is not inherently transcendent. It is not a rising above. It leans toward the immanent. Immanence here refers to metaphysical and philosophical theories of divine presence, in which the divine encompasses or is manifested in the madness (i.e. the material world), contrasted with transcendence, which suggests that the spiritual world rises above the mundane or material world. This isn't to say that a transcendent spiritual path is not at times a powerful antidote to inescapable suffering, or that a longing for the transcendent is not otherwise healthy, perhaps even especially for a mother. I have known the glory and beauty of this rising above. In one long season of my life, I would even say that it saved me. But for those of us who are no longer untethered, we need a mysticism that can stalk the wild shores of our daily lives. At the very least, we need a mysticism that is saturated in immanence and transcendence both. To combat hopelessness and a monochromatic schema, we need our eyes opened wide to our own unique daily dance with the divine, however chaotic, mundane, mulberry-stained and understated it may be.

So, this is a mysticism for those who love the world or want to love it more. It does not require a degree or a certain disposition, a religion or a church. It is not in creeds but in the prayers of the body as we move through the day. It is in the common moments we share – the collective experience of a train ride, kneeling to pick up puzzle pieces, the way sycamore branches click together like ice cubes in a glass. I do not want someone to tell me what the experience of the divine is or is not. And I do not want to tell you, either. But I want it. I scour my days for it and hope to come forth baptized both by what is and what is not.

Perhaps we do not have to find God as much as know God in our own hunger, in the reciprocity between nature and our bodies. If God is, then God is with us. All of us. We may not always know it. But we may spend our lives trying. And whatever happens or doesn't, it is still worth trying.

Stay

Within oneself very clearly is the best place to look; and it's not necessary to go to heaven, nor any further than our own selves, for to do so is to tire the spirit and distract the soul, without gaining as much fruit.

— Teresa of Avila [9]

How can I discover the divine in the roar of a train barreling through Sunnyside, my neighborhood in Queens, New York City, and in the way the steel rails screech as they halt at the 46th Street – Bliss Street stop? At this very moment, there is a long list of household chores and a (burning) pot of red lentils on my stove. How can I meet the Mystery by staying in my own body, my own life, my own clay? It isn't going to be easy. But I want to clumsily learn to plumb the depths of my daily life – to go within and down and deeper still to where the Mystery abides, bound within muscle, bone, sinew, ligament. I want to train my ear to hear the divine in the rare city-bound bird songs and to see the divine in the not-so-rare diaper pails and overfilled laundry hampers, the endless cycle of meal making, the cancelled babysitters and the not-so-balanced act of work, self, family.

Even more, I want to discover the sacred in the children I have, who are strewn across the world – two tiny ones under my roof, born of my body, and fourteen others, who are grown now and live in Armenia in a group home I started some years back for abandoned people with special needs. On a daily basis, I am half-buried in piles of dirty laundry and emails from Armenia. I do not have the luxury of retreating from my life very often. I do not even have the luxury of sleeping through the night. So, I have no choice but to begin here in this unlikely terrain for mysticism moving toward and within the connection we already have with all the world and with the Mystery.

This longing I have is not just a dream that is forever out of grasp. Simone Weil, a French philosopher, mystic, political activist and personal hero of mine, says: "He who is aching in every limb, worn out by the effort of a day of work, that is to say a day when he has been subject to matter, bears the reality of the universe in his flesh like a thorn. The difficulty for him is to look and to love. If he succeeds, he loves the Real." [10] The difficulty is to look and to love. Yes. That sounds about right.

That is not to say that retreating, solitude, and a longing to rise above are not valid spiritual and mystical paths. God knows they worked for me for a long time. For thirteen years, I took a week or two of solitude every single year. Holed up in cabins and occasionally on the beach, I did connect profoundly with the Mystery. It was never how I planned or when I wanted, but it was profound nonetheless. There were encounters that sustained and even saved me.

And there were times I needed nothing more than to rise above a particular pain or suffering or situation and experience the relief of a transcendent encounter. Those were rich years in some ways, but also lonely desert years. Solitude only happened once a year and in between was often a barren wasteland, especially given that I was not attending church and no longer relied on the communal cycles of liturgy, worship and communion in the same way.

But today, loving the Real is going to look very different. For starters, it looks like abandoning my frustration that I do not experience the divine as I once did. It looks like opening up my heart to the fact that mysticism can sink down to me; I do not have to rise. It looks like letting mysticism be what it already is – non-directional. And I hope it can come to me as I sit in this rocking chair, balancing my journal on one knee while the babe snuggles into my chest (while his diaper leaks all over me).

I want to discover that it can come to me when I sneak in some time to write poetry, in visions and day-dreams I sustain, in rapture and despair and frequent insomnia, in the 5 a.m. cry of the babe this morning for my warmth and skin and breast, in the spiral of worry when my child is sick, in the way I roll toward my beloved and search for his hand in the lonely hours of the early morning and in the impending rage when I have not had one mere minute in a day to be rather than to do. I want to love the Real in the way the sky changes with the rising and setting sun, even though I can barely see it sequestered as I am in this canyon of buildings and highways. This is how I want to live.

How I Live

What has melted of the snow
pulls through me in rivulets.

This is not about what I believe
but about branches that bear
down, clothed with ice.

I live with the same gravity—
pulled, melted, fierce

and bracket the ocean
because it is easy for longing
to make its own void.

God is a weight I did not expect.
I live where sun cracks the grey—

admit bewilderment
and grace.

Typically, mysticism has not been defined in the context of staying where you are, but rather is defined by stealing away, retreating, rising above your life. This concept is a common and ingrained assumption about mysticism for most of us, but one that is in direct contrast to most of our lives. This withdrawal is associated with a value toward the transcendent, which I have internalized, having been long tutored in religion, patriarchy and trauma.

But if this is an inherent quality of mysticism, I, for one, might as well give up any mystical longings in the here and now. Mysticism has not ever been consistently defined from the cracks of a commoner's life. It has not usually been defined by women either. The traditionally Christian idea of mysticism that I grew up with designated a "rare and advanced form of spiritual experience, not found among ordinary...folk. To attain to a state of contemplation men and women withdrew from the world and followed a way of life entirely different from that led by those who remained in the world." [11]

Necessity (one-handed typing and little creatures clinging to my body and forgetting to move my car for street cleaning) forces me in a new direction, a simpler and more inclusive path – one that means staying close to my own life, abiding within the confines of my roles and engaging in this tiring process of reclamation and decreation as part of communing with the Mystery.

Decreation, a term that Simone Weil first described, is "undoing the creature in us." [12] Anne Carson's book, *Decreation,* explores this concept as it relates to three female mystics, she says:

Each of the three women we've been considering had the nerve to enter a zone of absolute spiritual daring. Each of them undergoes there an experience of decreation, or so she tells us. But the telling remains a bit of a wonder. Decreation is an undoing of the creature in us – the creature enclosed in self and defined by self. But to undo self, one must move through self, to the very inside of its definition. We have nowhere else to start. This is the parchment on which God writes his lessons, as Marguerite Porete says.

I have nowhere else to start. And I am not willing to wait until my children are grown to encounter the divine again. I will have to find what I am looking for right here – in the middle of the city, and in the whirlwind that is life with small children, because retreating from all of this would be both impossible and at this point even inhumane.

There is a path of simplicity that we commonly associate with monastic orders and common mystical lore, but there is a simplicity that is even more radical. Each of us can walk the barefoot mystic's path whatever our lives look like. The call for simplicity demands the frame of one's own body, being and life to be present and unshrouded. All the ornamentations and distractions so easily become defenses against God and Self. That is one of the gifts of this season in which I find myself. Ornamentations are nearly impossible. It does us no good to have an idea of mysticism that includes images that are foreign to both our internal and external landscapes. We have to learn to see the divine as closer than breath, not belonging to another order.

Wake Slowly

This is not what I want—
strands loosed, frayed, wintered,
upon waking God lost
to me in circles of dream.

Sun refracts on snow.
Billions of points of light blind.
It can never be satisfied—
the mind. Never.

Water rivers off my sons,
puddles at our feet.

Is God only lost without love?

That is not the point.
That is exactly the point.

Every time we walk forward,
open-handed, everything
is at stake all over again.

The only real obstacle is oneself.

I woke this morning slowly leaking.
My newborn's milky breath, clouded,
eyes like wings closed to morning.

This yielding required even more.

There are mountains the mind
cannot peak and to try is to exploit it.

Let us partake: with bones,
with breath.

Geography

Where lies your landmark, seamark or soul's star?

— Gerard Manley Hopkins [13]

The early morning sun slants through grey sky, reaching over and under the elevated train track that is visible through the wall of windows in this local café. The subway trains rumble and roar past, in regular intervals, before they sink beneath the East River to the underbelly of Manhattan. There is a steady river of people crossing the streets, and then pooling together again while the cars pass through the intersection. Later today, that steady river will become a flash flood at rush hour and I will cling to the side walls, staying out of the way.

I wish it were not true, but I do not really want to be here in the city. All the natural metaphors and images that I fall back on to name and understand the world are foreign and out of place in this cityscape. My children do not even know *star* except in theory. And they are lucky if they get to see the moon's face once a month. They do not regularly behold the sun rising or setting on the horizon; they just know the shift of light in the narrow slice of sky above us as it turns from light to dark. Once in a while we can catch a glimpse of the setting sun reflected in a tilted windowpane on the flanks of these brick buildings.

For this and many reasons, I struggle to stay in this precise, prosaic moment, to stay in the book of my own body, in these particular places that are stuck or sore. Sometimes I wish it was still possible to try to rise above it all, as I did in my former life. But today I try to stay here in the caverns of my own mind, the corners brimming with memories, suffering, conversations, scraps of poems. I stay in traffic inlets – the pages of the landscape that are mine, and in today's pedestrian to-do lists, the sink overflowing with dishes, interrupted conversations and frustrations. Here the edges of my soul beg to be inhabited, even though I am weary and skeptical and have not slept uninterrupted for over three years.

I am compelled to stay in my own fault-lined story, knowing this story has a parallel life in the underground, which is also the beyond. For me, this all has to do with my work as a mother, a writer, and an activist. It has to do with the geography of exile – in the longing for home and its winding path. Exile is likely too strong of a word, given that I at least initially chose to move away from the mountains and I chose to leave organized religion. But then perhaps exile is exactly correct when it comes to the ways that my experiences have been sidelined in certain conversations due to my gender. But either way, exile is how it often feels.

I do not just live in Queens; I am trying to make a life here. Nestled in Queens is my neighborhood of Sunnyside, which to my mind is one of the friendlier cityscapes in the vastness that is New York City. It was built in the 1920s and 30s and is laid out in a fairly neat and tidy grid, with numbered streets and avenues, and mostly six-storied buildings. It was one of the first planned communities in the United States. You can discern that in the way there are shared green spaces behind our homes, and sweet shaded paths back into the trees. In many ways, it is a lovely place, but still so foreign from the forests I knew and the trees I lived amongst and the stars – the stars that sweep across the night sky like you wouldn't believe – in Northern Arizona.

But I am here – in a city where the outdoor gear I am accustomed to wearing is not a respectable stand-in for a wool jacket and snow boots have heels. Though I cannot adopt a wardrobe that consists entirely of blacks and greys, I have finally learned to dress in clothes punctuated with black. And I am learning to pronounce vowels differently. I have learned the arteries and mystery of the subway, and how to hail a taxi. I am learning. I am trying so hard. But I still need to memorize the blasted subway map so I don't have to reference it nearly every time I leave my house.

I have adjusted my expectations, slowly but surely and *quiet* now means the spring-green bud of the hyacinth. The wild is on scale with ant colonies, or noted in the occasional daffodil lodged defiantly in sidewalk cracks. It's in the sweet blues and reds of serviceberries I'm dreaming about through snowfalls – that we pick every June to eat on top of ice cream. It's in the abundance of plums that drop to the concrete in my dearest friend's back alleyway. It's not that it doesn't exist, but you have to lean over to see it or crane your neck to look up. And, you occasionally (blessedly) even step on it. But you have to slow down or it will likely never even register in your peripheral vision, much less your heart.

Here the skyscrapers are my mountain peaks – that which orient and guide my steps. Here the streetlights stand in for the stars in my night sky. And, like I said, there is no rising and setting of the sun, at least that I can see. Those are not the anchors on either side of the scales of my day. But I have learned to be a damn good judge of a covert sunset from twenty square meters of mid-sky. There are gradients of light and color that I thankfully can still register, lodged as they are between buildings. But there is no horizon.

I have been wandering through cavernous cities for most of the last thirteen years. I have moved too many times to count the city-blocks packed into my heart. My initiation into city life happened by choice but on a misguided dive from late adolescence into adulthood when I left the mountain town of Flagstaff, Arizona for college in Los Angeles. Even then, I knew that we each come with our own set of maps and that the topography of mine had to do with mountains, the relief matrix that leaves jagged the shape of the sky. Though I moved to Flagstaff as a child I know the truth of Ronald Blythe's words: "When do we begin to look? Or does the landscape enter the bloodstream with the milk?"

But in an attempt to leave a swirl of pain behind, I also left lupines, ferns, Indian Paintbrush and the largest contiguous ponderosa pine forest in the world. I exchanged all of these and more for a valley and tangle of smog, food and neighbors from all over the world and concrete. And as way leads on to way, I continued my city-based existence for the sake of love, not of the cities mind you, but for Aaron – the one who is now my husband.

We are all bound by something, often something frayed and tangled, even if it was chosen. For today, I am bound by the ropes of cityscape, grocery stores, family, work, and marriage, to name a few.

Extended Twilight

There are unrequitable lands I loved—
sparse forests, Indian Paintbrush, creosote musk.
Frontiers that matched my edges—
foreign rivers that muddied the laundry of my life.
But this is where I empty my days—
in the belly of a city carved out by subway cars,
between the rubble of exile and a stone hearth
smothered in matchsticks and primroses.
And is this Modernity—
prayers without roots, a brief tent pitched
between expectation and regret? Sun floods
the streets like seawater emptied against night
and there, orange spitfire inside a crocus bud.

What if I truly could leave behind the lands that feel irretrievable, where the sacred felt close and more natural? I want to dive headlong not just into the orange spitfire of a crocus bud but into the chaos of my every day. Both are here in abundance.

I want to orient myself within the feminine and create a spiritual home here – in this geography of motherhood and marriage, work and city. Some of the sense of exile that I am not alone in feeling has to do with the perceived distance of the divine due to the ways that relating to God have been largely and historically charted and influenced by patriarchy. Patriarchy, as a social system, harms all individuals, men and women alike. But in this system, and in my experience, women and children are marginalized and men's experiences are defined as the default paradigm. As a result, women are often trying to re-orient themselves to masculine schemas, often even unconsciously. And while the radical and intimate feminist face of God is emerging in our time, it is still hard to come by.

We are pressured to live only in the literal, surface and material realm. We assume that our selves are essentially separate and therefore competitive. [14] Even our view of power inhibits mysticism. Joanna Macy says, "The worldview underlying the Industrial Growth society perceives reality in terms of discrete and separate entities, which relate to each other in hierarchical and competitive fashion. Hence power has been understood as domination – power over, win/lose." [15]

If mysticism is about the awareness of our connectedness with all that is in the world and with all that is sacred within the world and within ourselves, we must abandon this damaging view of ourselves and untangle our understanding of power. What if power were simply the gift of participating with the divine, and allowing it to penetrate us through and through? In *The Divine Milieu*, Teilhard de Chardin says, "By means of all created things, without exception, the divine assails us, penetrates us, and molds us. We imagined [the divine] as distant and inaccessible, when in fact we live steeped in its burning layers."

To become aware of the burning layers is transformative work. That transformation may initially be public or private. But either way, it has an eventual bearing on the world, as mysticism implies dissolution of the inner and outer. Connection and oneness with the divine are sought for the sake of all beings. The work that any of us does individually is ultimately for us all.

Quotidian

The ordinary allows for the exceptional, but not the reverse.

— Kim John Payne [16]

My miraculous power and spiritual activity:
drawing water and carrying wood.

— Layman P'ang [17]

This morning I woke at 6 a.m. But lest that fool you, I also woke before that at 4:30 a.m. and before that at 1:15 a.m. and at 11:30 p.m. before that. But at that final 6 a.m. wake-up, I gave up and tiptoed down our creaky stairs so as not to wake the boys. If I wake them, I will hold them if they ask, even though Aaron is around this morning and perfectly capable. But if I'm honest, I first want a few minutes to myself – because even though most of my time is not my own, I still believe that the regular everyday routines matter and that it is these monotonous routines (both public and private) that make us who we are.

I feel my way through the dark into our kitchen, which is about four feet by seven feet long and graced with three or four families of mice. It is a tiny closet of a kitchen with blue and white linoleum that curls up in each corner of the room, leaving exposed slabs of hardwood that are impossible to clean. I gave up trying a year ago. The range is a miniature version. But for its tightness, there is a full-sized door with a window that looks out onto the shared green space. Bless the Garden City movement in England that impacted the planners here in Queens.

I look out the window, notice the first flowers of a belated spring – crocus buds and the snowbells – and take a deep breath. The kitchen is a mess, mind you. The sink overflowing with dishes we were too tired to wash last night. And in such a small kitchen, there is no countertop to stack them neatly on. But I take a few dishes off the range, turn a blind eye to the rest and heat up some water for tea. I put a slice of bread into the toaster and open up my round, sky-blue butter dish. (Since then, the blue butter dish has shattered on the floor and I may or may not have wept and said, "Why can't I hold onto anything beautiful?" But that is a story for another day.)

While I wait for water to boil and bread to warm, I open the back door to breathe in the light snow that spins through the grey morning sky. It makes heavy the earth. Spirals of light create webs in my mind. I can't help but smell the exhaust as well and part of me wants to slam the door shut, ward off the smells of city. But I don't. My eyes first land on a pile of gardening tools and buckets that I need to put away. I was over-zealous in my timing. Spring is not yet here. Two tiny dump trucks litter the yard, filling with snow. I should pick those up before the neighbors wake up. My mind jumps to a hundred things, large and small, that need to happen today. I try to force those thoughts back.

It can be hard to enter into quiet when it can be disrupted at any moment. It can be hard to even want to try for fear of being disappointed by the harsh jolt back to the world. But this morning, there is a hush that follows fallen snow. And I feel my soul slipping through the cracked-open door into morning snowdrifts. Steam pops in the pipes; the house creaks awake. My tea steeps and my toast is buttered. I close the door and tiptoe to the couch by the front window.

This window faces the tiniest of street-side gardens. Morning light streams through a window smudged and dirtied by little hands. But I barely see the smudges. It's the snow-dusted sycamores that line and buttress our street which capture me today. I shove a huge pile of laundry off my chair (yes, right onto the floor) and sit down. Time is of the essence.

I gather the fragments of myself together. Every morning I feel unspun, like a spool of thread come unraveled. I'm sure this feeling will continue for many years. But today the littles are still asleep. The house is small enough that I can hear their deep sweet breaths; they

are the anchoring of my quiet. I pull out my stacks of paper and ig-
nore the marginalia reminding me who to call and what to purchase
at the grocery story. It is time to write. I take one deep breath. The
deep breath whispers back. *Stay. Stay here.*

And then the quiet dissolves with the babe's wail, the frustrated
groan of my husband who wanted more sleep, and the pitter patter
of Jude's feet on the stairs, calling, "Mama? Are you here?" And even
though I am interrupted, my heart answers *yes.*

In *An Altar in the World,* Barbara Brown Taylor says that "earth
is so thick with divine possibility that it is a wonder we can walk
anywhere without cracking our shins on altars." I love this image as
I think of *need* – so palpable that I can almost touch it. Need is also
its own kind of altar. Silas, my babe, cries and it pierces through my
skin like love. The thin tapestry of solitude is ripped. His need is my
spiritual practice. Answering Jude's question is my experience of the
divine. My body is a mystical text. No one else can reclaim the spaces
within these walls.

And the truth is, I know some day I will miss this – not the quiet
but the way everything is turned inside out like pomegranates, broken
open, like hearts crushed open with bare hands – an offering to make
up for fatigue dragging through my veins. Where does it go – this
heaviness, this beauty? It weighs down the earth though the mass stays
constant. [18]

These are the prosaic sacraments of every day where one can begin
to locate the divine, even in the quiet dissolving.

Here

Snow flowers; spindles of light
twist idly in the mild.

I am unspun since morning,
since mother,

since not one
sentence, paradox, start

moves unimpeded toward
a close.

Even now I am pulled through
cracks into morning snowdrifts.

Need crawls toward the corners
and voices crisscross.

Each cry, each call darts into skin
and solitude is shredded,

a dust cover, it matters,
it doesn't,

until snow falls
and my tatters swirl in open air.

My miraculous power and spiritual activity, unlike Layman P'ang's, may be holding babies and sweeping the floor. It's not glamorous, that's for sure, at least not sweeping the floor. Rainer Maria Rilke is one of my favorite poets and a mystic in his own right, who viewed God as an intimate, and beyond all dualism of matter and spirit. Rilke says: "Discover that our way in the world is at the same time our way in God." Damn, I hope that's true. And some days, I also hope it's not. If my way in the world is distracted and joyful, harried and full and almost entirely taken up with my love for the boys and their immediate needs, and a vocation that suspends me over the Atlantic Ocean and a few seas between here and Armenia, then this fractured, stretched, bursting-at-the-seams way is also my way in God. And there is something in that that I struggle with. A part of me wants my way in God to be a place of respite, quiet, peace, like it once was when I took solitude every year. But if Rilke is right, this also may mean that the Mystery is found within my particular way in the world. And it doesn't matter one little bit what it looks like. That part is hopeful because I do not have to clean up the messy and cluttered house through which there is often not a clear pathway. And that is hopeful because it rather feels like God is often not here, because it often feels like my life is not sacred, but rather frantic and confused and landed like glacial outwash in the wrong geography.

I spend my days looking for a new way to see and know and hear the divine in the quotidian mysteries of my own life. [19] But it's hard and tiresome work. And as you can imagine, I often wish I spent my days knowing the divine in brooding forests or alpine tundra, my kids running wild rather than strapped to my body or into a stroller as we walk down the sidewalk and cars speed past. Doesn't that sound easier? But that is not for me, not now, and perhaps not ever. I live here, where my son takes joy in finding me seated by the front window instead of at the café down the street. I live here on a crowded street with neighbors from all over the world, where I get to hear at least ten different languages a day. I live next door to Paul and his wife, who is quickly declining with Alzheimer's. I live down the street from a dear nearly-blind man, Frank, who still walks the neighborhood every day and rests when weary by the noisy roadside on wooden benches. I live near Camille, who watches my babies when I work. I live near Jenn, who comes over once a week at the least with her daughter. We fold laundry and eat shortbread. I'm wedged in tightly between the subway station a couple blocks south and the Long Island Railroad a couple blocks north. I'm a few miles from the LaGuardia airport and airplanes constantly take off and land in our vicinity, much to Jude's delight.

I'm surrounded by speed and sounds and flight and frenzy. *This* is my book of common prayer; the pages are the bodies of my family, the thrown-together meals, the interspersed conversations and incessant questions: *Why are kittens shy? What is a hurricane? Why am I lonely? Can people who do bad things become kind again? Who is sad that baby Weston died? Can we go watch the subway and feel its thunder?*

In *Radical Wisdom,* Beverly Lanzetta comments that "Far from being unfocused, ephemeral, or rare, contemplation and mysticism are said to unveil the precision of reality as it truly is and to seed a person's consciousness with the ordinary and tangible presence of mystery in every facet of existence." If this is true, and I hope it is, then there is mystery in the litany of Jude's questions, in the disruptions, in the lack of sleep.

Try as I might to meet and know the sacred in the first still moments of morning, most of my days are not quiet. Most of my mornings aren't either, for that matter. Most of my hours contain the flurry of wakefulness and tears, squeals and meetings, trouble-shooting and tying shoes. Mysticism looks different for each of us because it calls us back, time and again, to the precision of our own lives, even when they are full of cracks. The precision of reality for me is in my writing and working. It's in soothing and building block towers – and in watching them fall. It is in the dressing and undressing, walking to the park, nursing, making meals, longing, pouring milk, washing dishes, nursing, changing diapers, holding hands, singing songs, nursing, waiting, asking, telling, yelling, praying, washing, nursing, wiping, sweeping, missing, scrubbing, nursing, hanging to dry, mopping, mending, drawing, painting, nursing, laughing, crying, holding, juggling, falling, flaying, failing, nursing, tending, zipping, reading, spooning, chopping, dreaming, blessing, nursing, picking, waiting, pulling, matching, cooking, toasting, clearing, nursing, stirring, flipping, boiling, simmering, roasting, nursing, kneading, needing, longing some more, attending, becoming, loving, hating, surviving, slipping, nursing, doubting, accepting, thanking, compromising, fighting, disappearing and appearing.

Fanny Howe says, "Every act is holy because every act is holy." [20] That's hard to believe and it is simultaneously a profound relief.

Renunciation

By our incantation we make and unmake worlds.

— Diane di Prima[21]

Even though men far outnumber women in historical mystical texts, there are some notable female mystics. But most of those women gave up family life to pursue a life where they felt free to participate with the divine. This was a revolutionary act for many of them. This allowed them the freedom to choose their own way. But from another perspective, it can be understood that female mystics were required to give up family life in order to participate with the divine. There is an ingrained and often unspoken and unexamined belief that the profundity of one's spirituality is correlated with what one has renounced, and this is compounded by the fact that spiritual people often appreciate challenge.

For most of my childhood and adolescence, I assumed the divine came closer to those who gave up something profound – whether that was a lover, a family, a certain vocation, money or security. Some people wake every morning at 4 a.m. to practice yoga. Some people sell all their possessions to feed the poor. Some people fast in the wilderness on a vision quest. And the truth is that often these practices do have value if they lead people into a profound connection with the Real.

I did my share of giving things (and people) up, in order to try to possess a God I have since learned cannot be possessed. I broke off relationships with people I cared deeply about any time I felt like they were becoming an object of passion and deep-hearted joy, for fear that this would separate me from the divine. As a teenager, I went on frequent mission trips – playing with orphans and building schools. One summer I was covered in so many mosquito bites that I was consistently feverish. I remember thinking that this suffering was what God wanted of me. Over and over I made the dangerous assumption that renunciation was a requirement – or a prerequisite – to knowing God.

I had internalized the voices that made sweeping sacred/secular distinctions – and sidelined entire areas of human life as base. I had bought into the paradigm that extreme self-denial was a pathway to God. This is understandable given that those who sacrificed much for God in a traditional religious sense have largely written the mystical texts. And it's understandable given that I have a somewhat radical streak in me and was raised in a church environment that praised and nurtured self-denial. But the divine is not relegated to the fringes or the exceptional. Mysticism is not inherently related to renunciation.

I have been slow – so slow – to realize this. I have been slow to understand that I do not have to renounce the world to experience the Mystery. In my own error of dividing the sacred from the secular, I was always starved for one or the other, depending on the season of my life. This destructive dichotomy has taken me years to recognize. I want a mysticism that repudiates extreme renunciation of self (to the extent that the self is lost) and is muddy enough to contain the world, the body, and the self.

But this idea of refuting renunciation is complicated by the fact that a more pedestrian life is still full of self-renunciation that, if understood correctly, can and must serve a purpose, providing a path of growth. So, in these pages and in this chapter of my heart, there is a parallel and a tension that I want to draw between the pedestrian and sequestered life.

Case in point: today Silas was beside himself – tearful, clingy, and desperate. He wanted to be held all day. Due to the cold, it wasn't practical to go on a long walk with Jude in tow, so I put Silas in the baby carrier and cleared a path by kicking things (literally) out of the way – angry, harsh gestures. Then I walked back and forth, back and forth, across our living room, across the grey wool shag carpet in the middle of the floor where Silas was born. I walked across the living room hundreds and hundreds of times. Jude eventually built his tiny circular train in my path, which I tried to carefully step over for the rest of the day.

Somewhere in between the hundredth and thousandth pace, the anger dissipated, Silas fell asleep, my back started aching and throbbing and I belatedly settled into the rhythm of the hours. I abandoned all my other plans for the day: clean the kitchen, read Jude a stack of books, take a shower. In my experience and inexperience, it is impossible to walk back and forth hundreds of times without losing one's mind *unless* it can be seen as a spiritual practice.

Once Silas was deep in sleep (or so I thought) and still strapped to my body, I lowered myself ever so slowly onto the couch to read Jude a long overdue book. He had been waiting all afternoon, impatiently, I might add, but who can blame him? You know what's coming next. You know.

As soon as I leaned back, easing the tense muscles in my back, Silas stirred and began screaming again. Not crying. Screaming. Bloody murder.

I screamed, too. It's true. So much for spiritual practice. And screaming didn't help at all. It was an animal scream that came from deep inside – not at anyone or anything except for the inability to calm and comfort my babe. It is a primal need – to be able to calm your baby. It can be, for me, an overwhelming need and when it is out of reach, every muscle in the body is pulled taut as a harp string. But the music is much less beautiful. I find it so difficult to love my boys well and as they deserve when I cannot help them or soothe their pain, which feels cruel. Loving others is by far the most difficult spiritual work. It is harder than any pilgrimage, fast or meditation practice.

While renunciation and sacrifice are not required in order to know God – as those of us who were raised within a strict religiosity may presume – they are a part of every life. There are grave sacrifices one makes in loving another person, in bending your dreams to get them to fit within a family. There are grave sacrifices in choosing to stay in the world and not retreat to a life of solitude and silence, liturgies and meditations. We cannot have it all.

But for a woman, this balancing act may be even more complicat-ed. Our roles and identities as woman, mother and wife have been closely linked to an unhealthy abnegation within patriarchal family systems and structures. Add to that, the foregoing of self that most women engage in when they become mothers is not considered bless-ed (although it is expected) by the patriarchy. It is not considered the kind of renunciation that brings one closer to the divine.

Moreso, undue sacrifice is the great archetypally feminine-orient-ed error, even though it is due, at least in part, to biology. I do not mean to disparage the beautiful and abiding sacrifices women make every day. But I do believe that women (and those who love them) must be careful that they do not overdo it. Given societal proclivities, combined with the fact that renunciation is a common theme within mystical literature, one has to be careful not to misunderstand or misapply it.

It will serve us to recall that the etymology of the word "sacrifice" is *to make holy*, or *to make whole*. With that meaning in mind, it may just be possible to push back and make sure that renunciation is a balanced force that is moving toward our wholeness or the whole-ness of the world. This brings me to the fact that I have given up the mountains and forests for over a decade for the sake of love. That may be fine. And it may not be.

But at the end of this long day that was a canvas for renunciation, I can set that question aside for now knowing I will return to it. My exhausted longing is to recast my life, the commoner's life, the wear-ing out the carpet to calm my babe, the animal scream that escaped from my gut, the glass of wine I am enjoying now, to see the Mystery therein, the mysticism of the every day. Mysticism is in the orbit of my main concerns, but I want the orbit of my main concerns to be a path of mysticism. I want it to be possible to make a nightly vigil of staying awake to nurse the babe. Thus far, I have not mastered that. But for this brief moment, I do see that it is possible. And I hold this fire-tinged world in my calloused and dirty hands so that the dancing flame of Mystery shines in my eyes, casting a glow over my prosaic ways.

Fragment

> *Though my aim is simultaneity and wholism,*
> *I don't know how to get there except by building from parts.*
> *Roles and processes – mother, poet, body, mind, word, flesh –*
> *may be discretely labeled but ultimately merge.*
>
> — Elizabeth Robinson [22]

I woke this morning bleary eyed and with a stiff back from nursing Silas all night last night. And despite my deep hopes, the nursing all night did not feel like a prayerful vigil or a mystical encounter. But I'm especially tired because I also stayed up late. Four women came over and we shared one too many bottles of wine. We shared Castelvetrano and Kalamata olives. We drizzled honey over the Camembert and plopped fig jam over the Manchego.

The four of us actually do not all live side-by-side in the waking world. We do not all share picnics in the park or fold piles of laundry together, though some of us do. We do not all come from the same background or country or understanding. But we come together monthly to read and to share. We come together to acknowledge that there is more to us than meets the eye. We come together to ask questions. We come together because the world sometimes threatens to swallow us whole. In coming together, we commit to try to bring all the parts and processes, roles and identities we hold and are and carry. I bring all my roles and parts – poet, body, daughter, activist, rebel, conformer, sister, folder of laundry, short-order cook, aspiring naturalist. We all need one place in the world where all that we are converges. We come together because we are mothers and we are women and we are searchers and we are stay-at-home moms and we work up to sixty hours a week and we are dreamers and we are idealists and we are pessimists and we are tired.

Last night, we read poems about the body, our frightful vulnerability, our bodies' landscapes of memory, love, generosity, oppression, childlessness or capacity to bear life. We wandered through our own limbs and organs and listened to the stories that our skin wants to tell. We examined the tethers of our knots, bumps, strength and bones. The body, I have learned, is never safe from the soul. The soul is never safe from the body. And while we each have disparate and differing worldviews, there was and always is a sacred texture to our conversations. The divine, as I understand it, was there with us in that candlelit room, uncovering our wholeness, revealing our tender scars.

Historically, whole swaths of our personhood including our flesh, and certain roles and processes, have been perceived as less mystical. But we don't want to succumb and renounce any parts of us even while it is chaotic and unruly at times trying to hold them all together. My friends and I circle and center and brood around some of the areas that have been typically excluded – mother, body, wife, sexual being. For me, it isn't easy to circle here especially when it comes to mysticism. It isn't easy to stay with the boring and messy, the everyday and common. Sometimes it is so much more tempting to try to be a radical. But this is my fertile ground. This is where I spend most of my days.

I doubt any of these women would feel comfortable calling themselves mystics. But whatever we call it or name it, whether we long for it or not, just below the surface of our lives is a silence, a deep core of divinity. It is always there – in the very bodies that hold us in this world. We just need to burrow into the folds of our lives. We do not need to travel far. We do not have to find God at all.

Yesterday I trudged back from the grocery store in a foot of snow, with Silas strapped to my back and Jude in the stroller and all the grocery bags hanging from the stroller. My arms were aching and I was pushing uphill. I stopped for just a moment to wipe the snot running down my own face and the stroller tipped over backward. The food went everywhere and Silas was crying and Jude was hanging upside down from the stroller and my hands were numb and cold and I wondered why I ever agreed to move to New York City especially while raising babies. Because who would want a life like this?

Given the debacle that is sometimes my life, I have no choice but to turn it all inside out, to look down instead of up, to look in instead of out. But I barely know how. All I know is that when it comes to mysticism, we tend to scour the grandiose and turn our backs upon the mundane. I do this. Every day. I want a way out.

Historically, we have looked more often to the powerful, to the strong, to the majority and to the dominant to define and articulate the spiritual life. We have also looked to ones who abide respectably and *by choice* on the fringes of society. But as one who is in the throes of "normality" and who works with people who live (not by choice) on the fringes of society and suffer hugely from this degradation, I know we have to look elsewhere in order to turn things around. We have to look far outside the realms and institutions of power and religion. We have to look in living rooms and group homes. We have to look to the powerless and those society deems weak and even dispensable. We have to look to the children. We have to look to the nursing mothers. These are the ones I want to learn from. Imagine the texture of mysticism as chronicled by someone with a disability or someone isolated in a nursing home or someone abandoned by their family. Where are these voices? If you are listening, I beg of you to speak.

I took two trains, over Queens and under Manhattan, and tripped and fell on the stairs emerging into distilled sunlight and cursing the living daylights out of this city. I look down at my shirt, which was clean when I put it on a couple of hours ago, but now is smeared with oatmeal and God-knows what else. I walk eight blocks toward Washington Park with as much dignity as I can muster to meet with my spiritual director.

Vivienne is a Sister of Charity – a nun of the order of St. Elizabeth

Seton. Seton was a mother of five biological children and many others besides. Maybe this is why, in my conversations with Vivienne, she is always bringing up the fact that I am a mother and a wife *as if* this has any bearing on our conversation about spiritual seeking and discernment in my everyday life. Despite all my waxing on about the need to bring all the parts of myself together, I struggle to do so. But Vivienne does not, and her gentle insistence is doing a silent work within me. She is unwilling to see me bring anything other than my full self to the altar, if you will, while I still hesitate to make room.

Part of this is the old resistance to see the mundane as mystical. Take, for instance, the subway ride here. It requires a deep shift in perspective for me to see the subway ride and the way other bodies hold up my body on sharp turns and when we screech to a halt, because we are so close, as mystical. Truthfully, I wanted to get out of there. It's musty. It smells. It's crowded and loud and clangy. But if I can just open my eyes and heart, God is here, in these sweaty bodies and heavily perfumed ones, in the ones who are in pain or struggle to stand up, in the tired eyes of the woman across from me and in my own frazzled and frizzy body and hair and mind. And if I can stay in this vein of thought and being, this very moment can become sacred. It is, in fact, already sacred, whether I see it or not.

So part of my resistance to Vivienne's reminder that I am a mother and a wife is that old way of thinking that I still butt up against to see the mundane as mystical. But I also want to preserve a sense of myself apart from these roles. And to the extent that I have bought in to the dominant culture, I imagine that part of that desire is rooted in the way our culture devalues them. Disagree as I might with the culture at large, I can still fall prey to this voice. I find myself annoyed at her insertions, "You have two children now." "You have sacrificed a lot for your husband." "You look exhausted." But the truth is, I was up nursing all night. I have lived in exile from forests and quiet and stars for the sake of my husband for more than a decade. And my two children break me open, in the best (and sometimes worst) of ways.

Motherhood is largely uncharted ground for mysticism. But I can only hope, despite and within my resistance, that the Mystery is here in the fifth nightly wake-up, in the bargains I have made with my husband, for good or ill, and in the way having a second child has spun me into a whirlpool of unrelenting fatigue and bliss.

This past summer, my family and I went to the Pacific Northwest. It felt good to escape the city, to be with family and dear friends. And it also utterly wiped us out – traveling with two children. We have yet to do it again and I imagine it will be a long, long time before we all get on a plane together again. But I hold onto the day we first arrived at Kalaloch, on the Olympic Peninsula in Washington. It was low tide – late afternoon. The skies were taupe-grey; the waters already charcoaled. The air was heavy with rain. The four of us wandered down to the water, barefoot, shaking a long car ride from our limbs. The car ride had been miserable and tearful as my children aren't used to car seats, having been born and raised in New York City where cars are so seldom used. Those people who say that their kids sleep so well and peacefully in the car, keep quiet!

The earth sloped gently when we reached the shore and there were thousands of square feet of water-logged sand, firm to run upon, glistening in the lowering sun, decorated with sea-crab bubbles. There were vast stretches of the liminal space between land and sea, where I am accustomed to only a small swath of tidal zone. There were occasional sea anemones grasping the rocks.

It could have simply been the ocean. It could have simply been a blessed moment in the wild. And it was both of those things, but when I tipped my perspective ever so slightly, that liminal space became our sacred ground. And our steps became our prayers, even while they remained our steps. In some ways, all that changed was that I stopped and took a deep breath before I ran toward the water.

Jude ran with all of his strength, pumping his short arms, his mop of brown hair splayed out like wings in the wind. The roar was tremendous and we had to yell to be heard. When we finally reached the water and were soaking our cramped toes in the breakers, Jude looked out at the vastness. He opened wide his arms and shouted, "*This* is the ocean. *This* is the ocean."

Yes, my dear boy. This is the ocean – in all its fierceness and power and gloom. In all its strength to give and take life. In the way it rushes through us. These are the ocean's prayers: this teeming swarm of movement, this freedom and vastness and depth. These are the ocean's prayers and these are ours.

"And those are the eagles…" he continued, embracing the sky and following the birds' motions with his arms. They were actually seagulls. We did not correct him. Sometimes the role of mother feels impossible to merge with the identity of mystic. And other times, oceanside, it is completely natural.

Sometimes all it takes is the simple power of looking and naming to recognize the sacred. I think that's what happened for Jude. It sure is what happened for me as I listened to him and looked out at that which he named in such a childlike fervor. The water was moody, the sky still light. We stood in the middle of the ocean bed. We stood and we knew God in just that water's edge way. The water's edge graced with my son's huge presence became my sanctuary. For a few blessed hours, I lived the life of a mystic who cannot steal away and who doesn't even want to. In other words, I surrendered.

Monasticism

May the time come when [women and] men, having been
awakened to a sense of the close bond linking all the movements
of this world in the single, all-embracing work of the Incarnation,
shall be unable to give themselves to any one of their tasks without
illuminating it with the clear vision that their work – however
elementary it may be – is received and put to good use by a
Creator of the Universe. When that comes to pass, there will be
little to separate life in the cloister from the life of the world.

— Teilhard de Chardin[23]

The monastic life is a way of life in which one renounces worldly pursuits in order to devote oneself to the spiritual realm. Shamans have this role in some Native American traditions. There is Jainism monasticism, the Buddhist Sangh and Sannyasa in Hinduism, to name a few. Monasticism is one of the many doorways to the mystical in multiple religious paths throughout the world. But in the contemporary Western paradigms that I am most familiar with, it often requires a profound renunciation of what is deemed "secular" – family, body, children, even oneself.

I know I bristle at this perhaps more than most. And I also know I am not the first to have been harmed by misguided religious ideals of asceticism and renunciation. For many years I valued purity above all else. Combine that with old inclinations toward self-punishing behaviors, and you have a bad combination. Case in point: when I was an adolescent and disturbed by a sin I had committed, I put the sharp and pointy cone scales of pinecones into my shoes and spent the afternoon walking around on them. It is no wonder I had to find a different way forward.

Thankfully there is always a way of protest available to those of us who have chosen and reclaimed ourselves, our families, bodies, and children. There is a possibility to create a spirituality that tears down the walls between sacred and secular. My way forward has been to adopt my home as my cave. My vespers are bedtime stories and spoken blessings over my children. My solitude is taken in half minute intervals while my children look at a nursery rhyme book and I sip a lukewarm cup of tea with dirty and crumpled hand-me-downs at my feet and an overturned basket of toys. I want the clear vision of Pierre Teilhard de Chardin – that all my movements and all my work in the world are part of a single, all-embracing work.

But all that said, I do understand the urge to live simply and ascetically within the orders of monasticism. And I want to be clear that I do not think that most monastics choose a path of renunciation for its own sake. Many mystics and monastics choose that path because of a deep and abiding love for the Mystery – that they want to stoke and kindle, that they want to give their life to. And I have that same longing.

If we allow them, the prosaic rhythms of parenting can serve the same purpose as monastic orders – to thin the veil between the human and the divine. Both ways break down our typical way of perceiving the world. I also have my soup to stir, bread to knead, laundry to hang, bodies to tend, matins[24] – that consist of singing a healing song to my children when they scrape their elbow, and evensong – when we light the blessing candle at dinner and together we sing: *Dear God, thank you for this food. Thank you, rain and bees. Thank you, sun and moon. Thank you, Holy Mystery.* Unlike a traditional monastic order, though, sometimes our evensong is interrupted eight times in those few short measures by a question, a complaint, a meltdown. Sometimes it's my meltdown, I have to admit.

One night, we were having lentils. My children hate lentils (though I continue to make them). They were crying and bargaining and complaining and despite all of that, I plowed through our blessing song, which only made matters worse because then I was not only angry that they were complaining, but angry that they were interrupting the blessing song. Sometimes it is hard for me to take the hint – that God is not in the blessing song, but in the ragged feelings and the disdain of lentils. It may be too much to ask that I feel the presence of the divine in annoying moments like this, but maybe the least I can do is *not* assume that the presence will be felt if I sing a blessing, or light a candle. That feels like it would be progress.

We have the vespers as well – a bedtime blessing which is a variation of a Jewish Shabat prayer that I offer my children with their goodnight kisses. I say it for myself as much as I say it for them.

Now I lay us down to sleep, in peace, Eternal One. In the morning we will rise to life renewed in sun. Spread over us the shelter of your peace. Shield us, guard us, clear our way throughout this lonely night. Shelter us beneath your wings as you fly close above. Safeguard us as we come and go in life, in peace, in love.

Let's be honest – the nights that I say this blessing over my children I am also interrupted at least four times, sometimes as much as a dozen. Usually, it's sweet and funny and my heart nearly bursts with love for them. But sometimes I lose my patience and sigh loudly and give up. There's a theme here around interruptions. Perhaps it's interruptions that are my entrances to mysticism. Perhaps the Mystery is in part that when we think we're reaching toward the divine, our intentionality gets in the way, but when we are side-tracked, interrupted, and even beaten down, we are more open to what is.

Speaking of interruptions, we (nuns and monks and fathers and mothers alike) all wake at regular intervals throughout the night, depending on the season. And we do it over and over again. The motivation of the monk's wakefulness and mine is attentiveness. We both are stoked, in our best moments, of course, with longing. I wake to nurse, comfort, soothe after a bad dream, worry. I wake to cuddle and snuggle. I wake and it is quiet but for Silas' tiny swallows (and the occasional siren going down the street or car alarm gone awry).

It is still except for Silas' tiny hands running back and forth over my clothes or skin until he slips back into sleep. I do not know where the nourishment flowing out of me into Silas' tiny body is coming from when I feel so bereft. At times I wake to my own rage and exhaustion. Sometimes it is so late or early both that I feel physically ill from fatigue. If there is a divinity of exhaustion, this is it. And it certainly does, like monastic rhythms, thin the veil between the seen and the unseen. And sometimes, let's be honest, it just makes you go mad. Exhaustion (like interruptions) makes cracks and in those cracks, we can leak out. And the Mystery can leak in.

Most often, there is nothing resembling prayer or mysticism in these nightly wakeups, but I can hope that life is a long and rugged prayer that can encompass even the most mundane of hours, even the hours when I only feel absence – the unilluminated spaces that are also companion to God. If, in these hours, I bring my full self to God – the angry, exhausted, desolate and wrinkled self – then it is still a prayerful awakening, even when I am full of rage.

I also sweep and scrub, knit and bind up, touch, teach, play, grow and argue, push and pull, tend and plant. And these are my sacraments whatever I deem the shape of my identity – whether *mystikos*, monk, mother, nurse or hermit. This is my chaotic holy ground. Can I stand here barefoot, stripped down, leaking vessel? Is this my burning bush – this the fire of my own tender and prosaic world – the mashing of bananas, the wiping up of spilled milk, the children's poetry, infrequent baths, an evening glass of wine with my beloved, the rise and fall of bread, the cloth diapers that never quite smell clean? Are you the Real? You, who hides behind the freshly washed sheets on the line that are already dirtied by little hands, who sears me with the look of my tender child, who sings a bone-song in the bare and clanging sycamore branches, who wakes me a moment before the babe cries out for milk? Is the sacred in these mysterious bio-rhythms, the shortened cycles of sleep, the art of worry, the bread that won't rise?

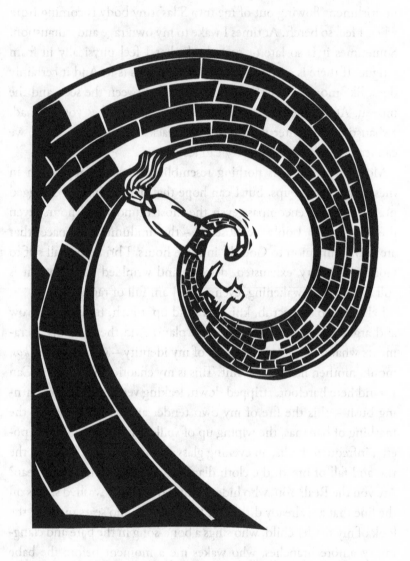

Baking Bread

Yesterday I formed wet dough.
Today it is flecked with flour
so my hands can work the soils

of yeast. You see—I live in cities,
landlocked. Each freeway circles
back on itself. Don't be surprised

to hear that electricity lines tangle
in my dreams. So my hands trace
each interstice of dough with fingers

meant for mulch and underworld.
I knead, back and forth, the salty
dough, the children's skin, until

there are very few fissures, cratered
though I am, full of divots. Yes,
I bake bread. I want something rising

and even more, to push my fingers
into earth's interiors. This is about
dark territories of abundance.

This is my rule, as stringent as any monastic rule. This is the maze in which I try (and often fail) to live gracefully. It is a new monasticism in its own right with all the requisite challenges and rhythms. But there is an important delineation between some ancient ascetic or monastic paths and the path of a parent. For a parent, asceticism is never valued for its own sake. The vows are biological. They are steeped in matter, in the body.

Marriage

Are not lovers ever pushing
at each other's limits? Lovers,
who promised each other
vastness, hunt, and home.

— Rainer Maria Rilke[25]

Most mystics who have written the historical literature and texts have been unmarried. Many of them have been celibate. The mysticism of someone who has chosen to be bound to another person in one way or another is undoubtedly shaped and affected by this choice. There is an interweaving of grace and sacrifice. In my experience recently, it is a daily practice to make and unmake, refuse and integrate sacrifice in a marriage, especially given the tendencies of women to sacrifice too much.

There is no denying that each life, whatever the shape, requires sacrifice in one direction or another. But sometimes recently I wonder if I have made sacrifice my default. Sacrificing is in my blood, in my ancestry as a woman, and sometimes it has been necessary to survive. But it may no longer be necessary in the same way. I keep circling around this thought: that giving too much and the ensuing loss of self may be one of the great feminine-oriented errors and may be one of the grim spirits of our time that we still have to reckon with. In *Women at the Well: Feminist Perspectives on Spiritual Direction*, Kathleen Fischer speaks to this, quoting an essay by Valerie Saiving in a book I have appreciated called *Womanspirit Rising: A Feminist Reader in Religion*. Fischer says:

> Contemporary theology, she contends describes the human

predicament as arising from separateness and the anxiety it occasions. Human freedom then brings with it the fear for the survival of the self and its values. Sin is the attempt to overcome this anxiety by magnifying our own power and knowledge. Love, on the other hand, is complete self-giving. Setting aside our own interests, we seek the good of others. Within this perception of the situation, sin is identified with self-assertion and love with self-lessness. Saiving challenges the validity of this definition for women, whose closeness to nature and cultural role of nurturing lead to a different kind of sin: lack of a clear sense of self, too much self-abnegation, diffuseness, and preoccupation with the trivial. However, spiritual literature is filled with a repetition of the traditional schema on sinfulness, and women's perspective is lost.

Only deep listening and tending to these terrains of sacrifice with brutal honesty will reveal the truth of whether or not a specific sacrifice is required, beneficial or not. There is no formula. But when things are no longer working, it is definitely time for renegotiation with ourselves, our children, our beloveds, our bodies, our communities, our world. From the micro-experience of my own family and broadening out into the greater world, I can see the evidence that on both small and large levels, renegotiations are begging to be had. And it isn't easy to know where to begin.

I know that it is important that one person not carry the bulk of the burden or sacrifice in our marriages or families. A lot is at stake – the kind of love I want to have, intimacy, equality, and mysticism, even. A feminine (or feminist) mysticism and a muddy mysticism at that, urges us not to choose a way in marriage (or otherwise) that completely crowds out one person or another. I think if we do that, we crowd out the sacred. As I have written before, the root word of sacrifice is *to make whole*. Thus, proper sacrifices can lead us toward the heart of the divine and misguided sacrifices can lead us toward our own pathologies and shadows. If the sacrifices I make are not serving the community of beings, including myself, it may be time to find a new way. If I am giving too much away, I risk fragmenting my own wholeness. Unless there is a self to bring to God, there will be no container for the revelation or experience of God.

In my own marriage, it is not black and white. There are a few canvases of sacrifice and receptivity that we paint upon over and over. One of those canvases is a cityscape. Aaron loves cities. He would live in New York City for the rest of his life if he could. We have lived here four years now and before that lived in Phoenix, Arizona for his Ph.D. program and before that Los Angeles. Between Los Angeles and Phoenix, we lived in Armenia. All are unlikely places for me to call home. But I have tried, despite knowing that I belong in quiet and in mountains. I am one of those people for whom it is hard to even survive in a city. But Aaron is a philosopher and he belongs at a college – teaching, studying, reading, and writing. And as fate would have it, his profession has thus far turned up positions in large cities. It would be a huge sacrifice for him to leave New York City.

Marriage is a long conversation and in our long conversation, we have been struggling to find the way that opens for both of us in regard to balancing these two needs of city (and maybe more importantly meaningful work) and the quiet of mountains. It has so far proved impossible to find a way that honors both of our passions. Today, I stand at the edge of myself wondering how much longer I can live in New York City. How much can I sacrifice in this way and still remain whole? Aaron has stood at the edge of himself too – wondering what it would mean to give up his identity as a professor and a philosopher. Both sides of the questions are terrible to behold. I hope that neither is required. How do we discern when and how to explore an edge? And when does it honor the Mystery and our own hearts to back away from those very edges? I do not know.

Sometimes our conversation around this issue ends in tears, occasionally in screaming, most often in silence, which is what happened last night when we were sitting on the big brown couch, a glass of wine in hand. We just made it through another round of applications and interviews in smaller, quieter towns but to no avail. And the last letter that started with "I am sorry to inform you…" was just opened (and grieved). So, for all intents and purposes, our hands were emptied. Mine were shaking.

I pulled my legs up underneath me and couldn't even look Aaron's way. We were both lodged in our own worlds of pain and our habits around the way they converge only seem to make it more painful. I suddenly found the passing pedestrians on our street fascinating and kept my gaze there. I could feel his leg against mine and in my peripheral vision, could see the way he opens and closes his hands when he is talking to himself, trying to make sense out of something, trying to explain something. I could almost hear the inner dialogue. *Well, let's try again in one more year. Well, I tried, didn't I?* I know it's not for lack of trying. And I say that, aloud, preemptively. But even so, I am not sure how much longer I can do this. It's the always waiting for the next thing that is sapping the life from me. It's not even just the city.

I didn't grow up in a liturgical tradition, but some of the liturgical practices have been a bridge to the Mystery when it felt like few bridges were left between myself and Christianity. One of the liturgical, albeit private practices, that has stayed with me has been Lent. Most years I practice Lent because I find it useful to set aside whatever it is that I discern is keeping me from connecting with the Real. Usually, I give something up, as is traditional Lenten practice. But I do not do so for the sake of renunciation, or at least not any longer. Rather, I do so for the sake of living with an unveiled heart. One year I gave up reading books for Lent because I was reading with an insatiable appetite and consuming books like they were chocolate. Another year I tried to give up spiritual pride. That was much more difficult than books. This year, I simply gave up.

I'm trying to hope that the bedrock beneath me is one of love. I am hoping that giving up will reveal something new. I have tried too hard to change my life – whether that be finding a way for Aaron and I to move forward, or trying to love the city, or trying to not be sad, or trying to not want so much. I have succumbed too often to the grim spirit that requires more of me than it should, that exaggerates virtue into something relentless and exacting, that asks me always to bend, always to give. Maybe (one can hope), by giving up I will find myself in the realm of the sacred.

Ash Wednesday

There is a steady stream
of cars speeding through me.

Lent asks of me, year
upon year, how unveiled

can I live. Fierce winds
thwart each attempt

to untangle the veil
that fractions body from holy.

But I am trying to stop
changing my life.

I am not giving up
chocolate for breakfast.

I am giving up.
I am living the cold.

Ice-blue ground,
snow dervishes,

hooded spinnerets,
winged and tumbling.

I beg: resurrect this
sharp-edged world,

brick and mortar,
my solemn shape,

full and leaking. I must
breathe, bathe, dress,

walk backwards until
I can slow this down.

Stop here. And when
I stare into night skies,

do not look for signs.
Look for invisible stars.

Maybe it is, in fact, time to err on the side of accepting my limits. After thirteen years of city life, of wandering, and rootlessness, I am coming to the end of myself. I am not totally ready to admit that out loud, but my dreams are speaking it over and over. This is terrifying. Just as it is terrifying to see the light drained from Aaron's face upon opening that last letter. Each year fewer jobs open in places that make sense for us as a family.

I want to step out of this identity as wanderer and giver and ask for a home. But tonight, I say nothing. I look out the window instead. Aaron talks silently to himself (and maybe me) somewhere in the deep recesses of his mind. And we listen to the deep breaths of the baby upstairs (he already snores). When his breaths are not even and regular, we are both startled out of our sad reverie. And then we quickly retreat again.

There was a time I thought that I would one day get to return home – to that smallish mountain town in Flagstaff, Arizona with a sky island nearby, the San Francisco Peaks. There I would have been in reach once again of family, red rocks, aspen groves, meadow rue, ponderosa pines and mule deer. And while this is still a vibrant longing, tonight I am not even thinking of Flagstaff, given the sacrifice it would entail for Aaron. As of late, I have hatched a new plan.

I want to ask for something in between – to move out of the city, to have Aaron commute into Queens, and to live in a town on the Hudson River, aptly named Croton-on-Hudson. While this is not perfect, there is some hope in this possibility. Even though we have talked about this possibility before, we were both hopeful it wouldn't come to this. Neither of us wanted a commute in the equation of our lives. Neither of us wanted to start over. I cannot bring it up tonight. The disappointment we both feel is too real and raw and I sense that we would become undone.

Instead, I get up and walk to our little kitchen. Aaron follows me and we begin to clean up, side by side, still not saying a word. I wipe down the oval oak table, the one that we have had since beginning our life together many years ago, the one that has been with us in seven apartments and one storage unit while we lived in Armenia. It is now scratched and well-loved, grimy and sticky and still not situated in a place I can easily call home.

Uprooted

Tossed between hooded cloaks
of night and the fire-lap of day,
between desert and stranger,

city and mountain, child and home,
sleep says in its downpour of dreams—
This is not the life I wanted.

Hands of ginkgo leaves are still,
silent after spring's coal-rain.
I am the only one left trembling.

Impatient with water-stained bark,
sun buried under leagues of clouds,
I want the ravage of light,

dancing breezes to strip away
the storm stuck to skin like sap.
I want to be hushed leaves,

to keep my heart in one place,
to burrow deep into the crust
of earth. Do I want too much?

Sometimes sleep is the windstorm
that uproots truth. My dreams
are thick with false indigo and sun.

Wandering

Sacred means necessary.

— William Kittredge[26]

I must remind myself that rootedness and making a home are not divorced from the mystical journey and neither is pilgrimage (or its kindred, the practice of wandering). All three can be mystical paths. Historically and even recently, pilgrimage has received a lot of attention. Journeys like the Camino de Santiago are once again in vogue. And for good reason. They are a powerful symbol of questing for the divine or the self. Historic literature more often portrays the wanderer as a man. But pilgrimage is a common spiritual practice in nearly every major world religion. The wandering figures in literature often illustrate the way an individual can wander to discover the divine and it is a common practice today even outside of religious spheres.

Aaron and I have erred on the side of wandering (albeit a tamer version of it) for the past thirteen years together. Our dreams have tethered us – whether those dreams be of philosophy or creating forever homes in Armenia. And those dreams have been no small thing. Even so, I have felt like an exile most of that time, whether because we have lived in cities or as ex-patriots living in Armenia. Sometimes we wander by choice and sometimes not. But there are so many good reasons to wander, only one of which is learning to measure the external landscapes against the internal ones.

In all of my wandering, I have sought to use the felt sense of exile as an opening for the divine. Landscapes that represented exile to me have fueled my poetry and my prayers. And these places, that I so begrudgingly lived in have now become part of my spiritual landscape. So, the value of pilgrimage and wandering is immense. I have experienced the fruit of these paths – and the freedom to find a new way after the spiritual path laid before me as a child was no longer working for me. But sometimes I am afraid that I will never shake this identity as exile, even when I am finally some place I want to call home. Sometimes certain identities take root and never let go.

My burning desire for rootedness increases with the years and now, two children later, it is holy and overwhelming. It is not lost on me that rootedness is more often associated with women in historic literature, which is perhaps why it has been explored less often and undervalued. But I want to see searching for a home and pursuing rootedness as an equally valid path to wandering in the search for God. It is perhaps not as glamorous (the pilgrims do get all the glory), but who needs glamor?

If I circle back to the themes of monasticism, I consider how rootedness is a monastic ideal in Christian orders, which I am most familiar with, but also in Buddhist and Hindu orders. In *An Unexpected Wilderness,* edited by Colleen Mary Carpenter, one essay talks about how the "Pilgrim and the monk depend on one another. The monk represents the human need for belonging and home, while the pilgrim represents the human need for autonomy and mobility… The monk tends to the home fires while the pilgrim journeys out in the world." [27] I am ready to tend some home fires. That's for sure. But first I have to find a home.

I have been driving up to Croton-on-Hudson every week or so to try to learn the lay of the land. And while it's mostly miserable driving there, as my children scream and struggle hard against their car seats, it is lovely when we get there. It is quieter. And there will be green and purple Joe-pye weed come summer. The air is cleaner. There is rushing water and space. I have been sitting in the snowy park near the center of town asking myself whether or not I could make a home here. On one of these expeditions, I found a blue house tucked out of sight on Quaker Bridge Road on the edge of town.

Yesterday, we all piled in the car to go up and see it – inside and out – together, for the first time. As we drove, I could feel the tension and the cage around my heart. Whenever we try to leave New York City, I struggle. Practically speaking, it's so hard to leave. I feel thwarted in this effort to escape because it's so huge and sprawling and crowded and traffic-jammed and often I start to feel more suffocated trying to leave than I feel when I stay on our sycamore-lined street. We were stuck on a tight freeway with no shoulder. The traffic was insufferable. The children were both sobbing in their car seats. Aaron was driving and even though there was nothing he could do to make things better, I felt myself turning on him. Sadly, I didn't hide it very well, unfair as I knew it to be. Eventually, I started crying and in between ugly sobs kept saying, "In New York City, they don't even let you leave."

Now I can smile as I write that, and I know someday I will laugh out loud, but for today the panic is still nearby.

It took Aaron and I awhile to work through the blame that surfaced in that conversation. I could feel his tension as well – his counting the miles on the odometer as we drove further and further from his college. I could feel him imagining the commute, imagining my bitterness if this didn't work out. And I hated myself for that very real possibility. I could feel his pull toward his job, his love of the city, all.

We try to be honest with one another, perhaps sometimes to a fault. We have tried to mine for truth and hold onto hope in this process. We have given up and surrendered and fought hard. As much as I believe that marriage is another container for mysticism, it seems like one of the more difficult ones today. It asks for daily efforts and presence in love and companionship. It is here, next to Aaron, that I confront the sacred, that I live out my doubts and my faith, my innocence and my failings. It is here we both come up against our own limits and the bounds and expanses of our giftedness. Marriage is no more or less sacred than a cloister. Like a cloister, you enter into marriage with desires, vows and no understanding in the beginning of how these will really shape your life.

By the time we arrived at the blue house, we were bedraggled and tear-stained. The diapers were dirtied and I was leaking milk. Aaron was worn out by my inability to hold back my disdain for New York City (forgive me, those of you who love it and call it home; I actually envy you). When we walked through the house, we didn't fall in love or anything, but we could imagine making a life there. I thought it was blessedly quiet. Aaron missed the constant rumble of the city. He didn't say so, but I know he did.

I'm not sure how we got from there to here, but we put an offer on the house and now we wait. I am afraid. I am afraid of the sacrifices it will require in both directions this time – the commute for Aaron (and what that also means for my work schedule) and starting over again still so far from friends, family, familiarity. I am afraid that our tension will not dissipate but rather will follow us here. I wonder if this place will become home. Even though I am not sure, in the Venn diagram of our marriage, this is the only place of intersection that we can see.

In marriage, we give and receive – sometimes too much, sometimes too little. It feels like we live and try to love and often fail miserably in a half-lit room. I want to throw the curtains back and let in more light, but every time I try, I realize that evening has already fallen. It has been moonless for a long time.

My spiritual director keeps reminding me that sometimes we sacrifice for the wrong thing. I don't yet see exactly what she means as this relates to my life. I wonder if she is implying that by moving to Croton-on-Hudson it would be the wrong sacrifice. This thought haunts me, but I see no other way forward. So, I push it down and wonder if maybe someday, the house on Quaker Bridge Road will become home. Stranger things have happened.

Common Refrain

It is time to follow limbs pressed flat
against a snow-cold wall. March breaks
down winter after a decade or more
of exile. Tracks steel toward candled
horizons I must arch along. Does lichen
cease ruining each winter? I am searching
for one short day without devastation.
Composing reparations while the forest
mends herself. Road of lungs, intestines,
veins that know the way, I have never
followed you by the light of day, cut off
the hand that reaches for nostalgia and
instead, chosen a home.

Trying to buy this house (and our first house) on Quaker Bridge Road has turned out to be complicated. The house needs a lot of work. There are two major environmental hazards on what looks like pristine, peaceful land. Endless horizons of tasks that require the work of our collective hands are one of our precise marital poisons. Perhaps this is what happens when a philosopher and a poet wed.

But in our effort to let more light in to the darkly lit room that has become our marriage, we do not want to bring an overflowing cup of poison to our table. We are trying to buy a house to support and strengthen our union after a long season of rootlessness. I fear that this endless list of home improvement projects will hurt us. But if we could get through it, we would have a simple home on a gorgeous half-acre. Aaron would still have a job. I would have some quiet and maybe the boys would even have some stars.

It's easy to imagine the divine in that quiet and in those stars. It's what I know. It's how I'm wired. But where is the divine in the here and now? Perhaps the divine is in feeling out our own edges and those of our marriage. Perhaps it is in searching for a way forward that honors those edges. What is the way of peace? A dear friend told me the other day that she hopes for a gentler way forward for us, even than this. I hear the longing in her voice and I have the same longing, but I think I've given up on a gentle way.

We are feeling around in the dark. Decisions often are like that. My mother says that you should not make decisions when you are tired or stressed (we are both). I agree with her, but what about those times when you have no choice? I can only hope that sometimes when you are stressed and tired the truth is revealed – the truth of limitations. And sometimes the truth of limitations is just as powerful as the truth of possibilities.

Speaking of edges, it feels like I will never have solitude in the mornings again. I have what feels like a never-ending cold and have been so sick that I cannot pull myself out of bed on time. Silas was up, wide-awake up, for two hours last night. He wanted to nurse and fling his tiny body over mine and curl around my neck and heart. As beautiful as this closeness is on some days, I am at a limit of what I can handle and am teetering on my own edge. Can I back up from this cliff?

As if in answer to my questions, yesterday the blue house we were trying to purchase slipped through our hands. The sellers moved on to another buyer in an effort to find someone who would not be concerned with the environmental hazards. If I am honest, I am mostly relieved even though this means that making a home is delayed once more.

Today I wish that mysticism, or the life of the sacred, meant I could leave all of this behind. I wish the sacred weren't in the grit and dirt and in what feels like my useless desires for something different. I wish it weren't here in the tears and in the sense of exile.

City

> *Look, it's spring. And last year's loose dust*
> *has turned into this soft willingness.*
>
> — Mary Oliver [28]

Today spring is undeniably here. The snow will not visit us again, until next fall or winter; it will not dampen the earth or the noises with its wet grace. And willing as I might be, it remains challenging for me to stay grounded and embodied in this conversation around mysticism. My temptation, time and again, is toward the lofty. It makes sense then that it is a parallel challenge of mine: to see the face of the divine in the cityscape and not relegate the Mystery to pristine and wild places. Even for agnostics there is an experience that sometimes accompanies untainted and wild earthscapes, which can be interpreted (or not) to be a Presence. But in the city, at least for me, it is a different story. I don't want this to be true. I envy those for whom it is not.

In James Hillman's essay, *Anima Mundi,* he talks about the soul-spark of man-made things:

Let us imagine the anima mundi as that particular soul spark, that seminal image, which offers itself through each thing in its visible form. Then anima mundi indicates the animated possibilities present-ed by each event as it is, its sensuous presentation as a face bespeak-ing its interior image – in short, its availability to imagination, its presence as a psychic reality. Not only animals and plants ensouled as in the Romantic vision, but soul is given with each thing, God-given things of nature and man-made things of the street.

I hope it will be possible to come to know this aspect of the sacred, even as I am trying with all my might to leave the city behind, maybe especially as I'm trying to leave the city behind. I do not want to lose this chance to expand the way I can know and love the Mystery. My children teach me a lot about this aspect of the divine, fascinated as they are with tall buildings, construction sites and the machinations and movements of modern construction technology.

City Face of God

Each metered block
sold its skin.

Colors clang.
Steel rods pierce sky.

A crescent moon
dips behind graffiti.

The sky has lost.
Sirens shake single panes.

Clamor of need, noise,
greed, God.

On Ash Wednesday
I gave up

dawn and hush.
Subway rails screech.

The train lurches
forward and need

presses against body.
We hold each other

up by sheer proximity.
Hands have nothing

to do with it except
I didn't mean to read

absence into what we make
with our citied hands.

Although I understand on a theoretical level that the landscapes (both literal and figurative) in which mysticism thrives are as multiple as the individuals who employ them, it is hard to translate this into finding my own mysticism of the city. Living in Queens, I have been starved for the face of God I once knew as a child – the God of the enclosing presence of the forest, tucked all around me, and the orienting and imposing God of the mountains. It is hard for me to survive on the screech of trains, sirens each night, incessant noise and only irregular glimpses of the moon. These are not lofty or pristine places but regular run-of-the-mill city blocks, chock-a-block full of Presence that I cannot yet identify or experience. I wonder if that is because the mysticism of the city circles around Absence. Maybe by seeking Presence, I'm missing what is here.

If I'm on the right track and mysticism can be muddy, if every act is holy, then the divine is not excluded from any part of life (or death) and the face of the sacred is here in the tired and sagging sidewalks, in the panoply of greys, in the flit and flight of pigeons, in the absence of clean air. But. But I can't feel it. I only feel Absence. I imagine the hem of God's skirt brushing over these crumbling streets, but it is still only an act of imagination. I imagine that even these crumbling streets are a sign of the Mystery, but everything in me protests.

The one blessed arena where I feel like the face of the Mystery is easily accessible to me within the confines of the city is through humans. And goodness knows, there are a lot of us here – over eight million to be exact. I can feel Presence in the man screaming on the corner, in my small child learning to walk and step over the cracks in the sidewalks. I can see God in the downcast gaze of my dear elderly neighbor with Alzheimer's and her exhausted husband. I can see God in the high-powered attorney walking down Fifth Avenue and waxing on dramatically on his Bluetooth. This is where the theology of incarnation has irrevocably influenced and captured me. Mother Teresa taught that "Each one of them is Jesus in disguise."

I long to leave the city. I didn't think this was permissible for a long time. I felt like I had to be able to make it work – that this should be possible for me. Now that expectation is loosening its grip, but for today, I am still seated in a small café under the Seven train's iron tracks on a grey-streaked street fighting to see that the sacred encompasses and embraces every last place – brooding and sun-filled, devastated and cultivated, wild and sinking, raped and protected, innocent and ashamed. It's not an easy fight. But is it possible that even here, in this place that I cannot seem to be rid of, the heart of God pulses and throbs, beats and skips a beat?

Last night, Aaron and I toyed with the possibility of him leaving his job and moving to Flagstaff. It would be a huge loss, perhaps a devastating and irrevocable loss, and honestly, I can only ask questions about it for now. It sends him pacing back and forth across our creaking living room floor, over and over and around that same grey-wool carpet. It keeps him up at night, trying to imagine another life, another job, another role, when this one fits him so well. I don't want him to have to find another vocation. It is almost as if I can see his heart breaking whenever we talk about it, breaking open and into a million pieces and irretrievable after that. We are both doing our own reckoning.

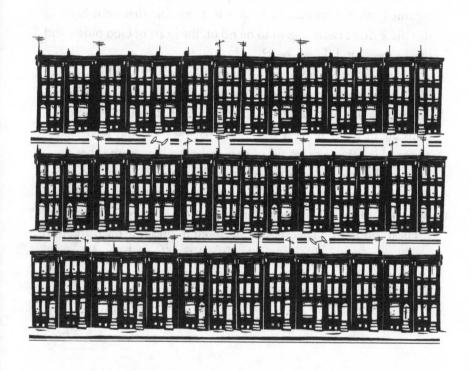

Reckoning with Queens

I cannot etch cityscape stamps
onto skin when I have not been
to the Unisphere and don't know
if the Seven train means chapters
read, night owls, staph or
something like you-against-me.

In this museum of the moving
image all my metaphors have
turned to steel, horns, grind, air-
like-stickers, donuts, a child's
strawberry-filled hands. I sneak out
after dark, clip choking ivy.

What would happen if we slowed—
and lost—I cannot help thinking—
dandelion clocks ticking away
seconds, water fields cloud-stamped
with autumn, wind the only traffic,
no train to whip through night falling.

If, God forbid, Aaron does end up leaving his vocation, if this version of loss is ours to bear, what will happen? Will there be any shred of collective hope between us or will we fall even deeper into despair? It could easily go either way.

Matter

Let us establish ourselves in the divine milieu.
There we shall find ourselves where the soul is most deep
and where matter is most dense.

— Teilhard de Chardin [29]

Consolation of Matter

Dark fragments into voices
of buried bulbs

or is it scraps of starlight
leaking through blinds?
The windowsills are wet
with longing, a long night
of breath. The children
crawl between us,

their weight, a relief.
After the syntax of dreams

constructs the distance
of God, their crowding

is an argument against
my invisibility,
their whispers braided with
buried tulips and

stars unseen for city lights.

When I look back over my life, I see stark evidence that I have been confined to the realm of Spirit – the transcendent. And for some time, I have been furiously trying to break free of this containment and to descend into matter. I wonder if the same is true for God. I am learning what it means to stay with the immanent and see the sacred here. Immanence here refers to metaphysical and philosophical theories of divine presence in which the divine encompasses or is manifested in the material world contrasted with transcendence, which suggests that the spiritual world rises above the material world.

I don't want to skip over skin or matter any longer. The word "matter" comes from the Latin word "mater," which also means mother. Matter is the shadowed Mother who has been rejected in many modern religions; for so long I have rejected her too. Matter has been the ugly stepsister of religion in so many ways, and disconnected from the conversation of mysticism. In our traditional prayers and religious practices, the tendency is to rise up rather than sink down. But these days I am tethered with strong cords when I try to rise up. I have no way to reach, weighed down as I am with two littles. And even more, I don't want to reach away from this world. I want to love the world more. I want the gravity to be Eros. I want to want to be here, even when the here means Queens.

I wonder if staying with the immanent begins with breaking down the separation of body and soul or even in inverting the ways we imagine these entitities. In *Anam Cara*, John O'Donohue, an Irish poet, priest and philosopher, writes about how the soul is not within the body, but that the body is within the soul. O'Donohue says that "your soul reaches out farther than your body." I know that to be true when I listen. What if I could live as though the soul, as the outskirts of the body, was always in contact with the world and this was our portal to the divine? Then, would I feel so lost?

I was taught through the schools of religion and sexual trauma to leave my body behind. These two schools reinforced one another and reiterated the same message. In order to survive trauma, my early apprenticeship was in elevating Spirit. A common move that the soul makes to survive trauma is to disassociate – which can be experienced as rising above the body, even seeing the body (or what is happening to the body) as an illusion. This blessed coping mechanism can turn dismal and detrimental, but in my case was reinforced in traditional Christianity where the highest goal is to leave your body behind and unite your soul with that of Christ's. I am engaged, along with so many others, in undoing the years of schooling, and learning how to inhabit my body as I did when I was a child. I am uncoupling mysticism from the denial of the flesh.

All that I can manage these days is to descend into the book of my body and stay within my sense-based experiences – believing that firmly establishing myself in the realm of matter will facilitate, rather than impede, a mystical connection with the Mystery.

This is the heart of God – the way the sun just broke through these single-paned windows, and in the washing of my hair this morning while Silas played with a tube of toothpaste on the bathroom rug.

In this journey of the reclamation of matter, I am profoundly influenced by a dear friend who recently converted to Judaism. Judaism, as I understand it, does not encourage the typical monastic ideals and visions. Given that I am already leaning toward a more rooted and muddy spirituality, there is so much about Judaism that makes sense. The movements of the Torah's commandments are blessedly aimed at purifying and making sacred the physical world. Abraham Joshua Heschel, a Jewish rabbi, says:

Judaism is a theology of the common deed...dealing not so much with the exceptional, as with the management of the trivial. The predominant feature in the Jewish pattern of life is unassuming, inconspicuous piety rather than extravagance, mortification, asceticism. Thus, the purpose seems to be to ennoble the common, to endow worldly things with hieratic beauty; to attune the comparative to the absolute, to associate the detail with the whole, to adapt our own being with its plurality, conflicts and contradictions, to the all-transcending unity, to the holy. [30]

I have been changed and bolstered by these ideas. I want *this* to be the way I devote myself to the Real. I want a mysticism that includes every single act and every single bit of matter.

The gift and mysticism of matter asks that we notice the divine in our communion with flesh and blood, the experience of a sunrise, the twittering of birds if you're blessed to be in the wild, in our experience of the exhaust of the Seven train as it barrels past, in the sensuousness of this baby asleep and draped across my chest, warm and breathing, and in the times when he is crazy with fatigue but fighting it, and butting his head against my body. The mysticism of matter asks that we treasure the world – its oceans and ordinary seagulls. The divine is present in the bread and butter of right now though today, I wander around the underground in the tangles and piles of soil and wire.

I am obsessed with the medieval mystic Hildegard of Bingen. I love that she is considered "The Unruly Mystic." I can most definitely relate to that. From the Rhineland, Hildegard spent most of her life as an abbess in a hilltop Benedictine abbey she founded. I cannot relate to that.

She was the first identifiable composer in the history of Western music. I often turn on her chants as a backdrop to my days, especially *O Ignis Spiritus*. [31] I do not know that there is any landscape, person, mess, or ruin that is not changed or disassembled for me if I am listening to her music through that encounter. It is not that her music alters the world. It is not that it even makes things better. But it alters how I perceive the world and allows me to enter more deeply into what is frayed or chaotic. It is a reminder that all of *this* that I behold and bear is part of the Mystery.

While none of that sounds particularly unruly, Hildegard was also a revolutionary. She was brave and overbearing. She was an artist and a sensual lyricist who wrote both medical treatises and poetry. She was a feminist before there was such a term. She was a naturalist who chronicled the ways in which she used plants to heal others. She loved animals, plants, trees, stones.

She began having visions when she was three years old and wrote many of them down. These images primarily served to deepen her love and respect for humanity; she saw human beings as sparks of the divine. While her incredible sight and moments of transcendence interest me, I am most captured by her claim that the most important aspect of her life was that she tended bodies, and used the curative powers of herbs and the earth to do so. She treasured the world in a way that I strive to. And she was able to hold both the immanent and the transcendent simultaneously and live from the spaces where they intersect.

What Makes Life Holy

The boys greeted him—one with tears,
one with spinning. It is hard to hold love

within the folds of the body, thirteen years
of marriage, the way I sweep four times

a day. There is something ascetic to this
life but that is not what makes it holy.

Say the same for pleasure, inverted.
Pleasure is holy, though it is not what

makes life holy. You see—sycamore arms
reach through the maze of shine, cerulean,

cloud. But their work is underground
in tangles of pile, soil, wire. Holiness needs

the body—the spilling out and over—
whether from love, asceticism or pleasure.

To remember, think of Hildegard's many
hands. She did not claim it was her visions

that healed but rather gold topaz for loss
of vision, aloe for jaundice, geranium

for colds and emeralds for heart pain.

When my longing for a connection with the divine feels impossible, disappointing or complicated, I am trying to explore and make space for connecting with my body, the earth and other people, believing and doubting both that these will not only lead me to the sacred but that these are in fact sacred. Seeing the unity and simultaneous multiplicity of all things as holding the sacred is a paradigm shift that, as Beverly Lanzetta says, "subverts the notion of a distant deity." [32] This realization has astonished me. After accepting the idea of a distant deity for so long, I am unraveling with this former construct – unraveling into a blessed unity, and deeply grateful to no longer feel locked out of the heart of God and the soul of the world.

This week, it is part of my spiritual practice to learn the flowers of spring, and in doing so, I think of Barbara Brown Taylor's words: "You also remember where you came from and why. You touch the stuff your bones are made of. You handle the decomposed bodies of trees, leaves, birds, and fallen stars. Your body recognizes its kin." [33] Today I try to recognize my kin in crocus, daffodil, snowdrops. It is part of my spiritual practice to go out in the rain without an umbrella, to *be a body* in this thereotical and post-industrial world. It is the path of mysticism to memorize the body of a beloved – to know what the muscles in his or her face do when buttressed up against despair. It is muddy mysticism to understand how the plants in my tiny container garden gather bees or butterflies (or threaten them). This is a work of excavation.

I consider the possibility of uniting self and earth. I long for the earth around me to be part of my own body and being, not consciously separate. I see this work as a gathering up, as an act of restoration and holiness and reparation and of course, mysticism. This world (and my own heart) is so fragmented and divided; perhaps there is nothing more revolutionary than one woman or man who stands barefoot before the tender heart of the universe displayed in the vivid colors and textures of matter. This is a relief. This, I can try to do, especially when my mind cannot cross the channels of intellect, creed, dogma and belief.

Teilhard de Chardin artfully braids the spiritual power of matter through much of his work, beckoning me toward a new way: "Bathe yourself in the ocean of matter, plunge into it where it is deepest and most violent; struggle in its current and drink of its waters. For it cradled you long ago in your preconscious existence; and it is that ocean that will raise you up to God."[34] It is not just people who need to be reminded of their beauty and their indivisibility with the Mystery, but also land and flowers and city streets and rivers. We, as human souls and bodies, will not experience our sacred nature and our unity with the Mystery unless we seek to reclaim all matter as a part of that divinity.

The world, like man-made objects, has a soul that wants to be reclaimed as sacred, along with my body. For all of my life I have been at ease in the natural world. I spent much of my childhood and adolescence seated in the forest, in a circle of trees, leaning against one beloved tree, singing my heart out. I wandered the trails behind our home at sunset and sunrise, alone and accompanied. I slept on the trampoline so I could see the stars. I laid flat in the small hollow near the house, cupped in the hands of a small meadow, baby ponderosas pushing through the soil around me. But I valued the natural world not for its own sake. I valued it for my sake and for being a conduit to a purely transcendent God. But I see it now differently. In light of the wholeness and unity I am coming to perceive, the distinctions between God, natural world, and other people matter less and less. The city, the waterfall, the flower, the body want to be listened to with rapt attention and care. The sacred is *this* close.

When I walked down my street today to grab a few groceries, I placed my hand on where I imagine the heart of the sycamore is in front of my house. I leaned my head back and looked up through the crown of bright green-yellow leaves. I listened to the rush and swirl and dance. I thought about the people I love in Armenia. I thought about my children, my husband. I felt all the branches of my own existence as I leaned against the creaking trunk and let solace pass through me. The sycamore and I are reaching and growing and changing because of this city. The sycamore has a four foot square plot of earth from which she has to gather all her nourishment. Otherwise, concrete surrounds her and hems her in. But still, the sycamore thrives, creates shade for my home and is home to many small creatures. There is a shift happening in me, a metamorphosis, I hope, in which I am awakening to my own body and also to the bodies of the sycamores.

Now I am ready to tell how bodies are
changed into other bodies.

To better survive concrete and smoke,
the native sycamore was crossed

with an Old World. Lost in the transfer
to urbanization, my name changes

as the plane tree's. Time requires
my body as a sacrifice. Or is it love?

Most century-old sycamores are
hollow at heart, not by scythe of city

smog but as a shield for swallows
and swifts. Their bark gleams

like picked bones at midnight, clicking
to the tremors of the blizzard. This

is how I console myself along with
the fact that sycamore wood is almost

impossible to split. Yesterday I saw
an aged plane tree at the butcher's,

a bloody block, atoms still tightly
wound, endlessly hacked. I thought

of how it didn't stand long enough
to become a hive for swallows and

squirrels but bleeds now through
other skins. After not eating meat

for years, I bought a rack of lamb.
The butcher tucked it in brown paper

made a swift knot of twine and
wiped the blood on his apron.

Gather

As the experience of oneness with God, mysticism is the radical substantiation of the dignity of the human body.

— Dorothee Soelle[35]

I have a feeling it is going to be the work of the next few decades to recover the world of matter as an entrance to mysticism. It requires intimacy and patience. There is matter to be recovered outside of oneself (that which we live within) and the matter within the confines of one's own body – a gathering up of oneself into a whole being of spirit and matter, body and soul. Iris Marion Young writes about consciousness and subjectivity residing in the body itself, a concept she finds useful because if you can situate subjectivity in the lived body, then dualistic metaphysics are challenged and jeopardized. She writes that the unity of the self is a "project sometimes successfully enacted by a moving and often contradictory subjectivity."[36] Pregnancy was one of those projects for me. It completely altered the structure of the self.[37]

When Jude, my first babe, was born, I was astonished by the way my body would wake in the middle of the night mere moments before he woke to nurse. Where did the structure of myself end and where did he begin? There was a physical reciprocity that I had never before experienced. Even when a few city blocks separated us, I knew he needed to nurse by the way the milk came rushing in. There were a few times when I was away and knew, deep inside, that he had begun to cry. And I learned later that I had been right. Before his birth, I had never known the terrain of my body or selfhood to alter and metamorphosize in such a profound and fluid manner.

The most intimate matter is that of our own bodies. I look down at these large hands of mine as I write. I used to hide them in church because they felt so imposing, resting there on my legs like everyone else's. I have learned to love these hands that can hold so much, their breadth and strength and muscle. I look at my freckled arms, and the skin that is just beginning to wrinkle around my eyes, mouth and brow from smiles, laughter, worries and concern. And I see this body, at least for right now, as lovely, and another portal to the divine. But I have had to fight so hard to see it as such.

I wonder: is this seminal act of loving oneself (including one's body) one of primary challenges of a feminine mysticism? If it is correct that one of the great feminine-oriented errors is to give too much up, if this coping mechanism is embedded in our female ancestry and we too often buckle under this inherited weight, then perhaps this love of the self and the body may be part of the antidote, the way we push back against this grim spirit of our time. Even as I write this, I bristle at the ways I struggle with the contemporary self-love talk. And I want to distance myself from a practice that can feel almost trite. What I am speaking of is not trite. I believe it has to do with bestowing value where it has not been granted historically. I believe this has repercussions for issues of justice and equality as well.

I believe it is important here to speak of body, earth and universe as "thou" rather than "it" and I am trying to make that adjustment in my speech and writing. I have been influenced by Martin Buber's I-Thou concept, in which the other is not separated by discrete bounds but is in living relationship with the I. Our bodies are trees of life – reaching roots down into the rich soil below and reaching limbs to the heavens, simultaneously embracing soil and sky. Our bodies are not an "it" outside of ourselves. They must not be relegated to the status of "other."

These animal and earthly bodies are some of the many canvases upon which we paint our mysticism. They are the skins through which we can know and touch the divine. Is it possible that the body is the most natural bridge to the divine and that the chasm between the two was carved by dualism, patriarchy, misguided religious ideals and even trauma?

Becoming a mother was the start of a purification ritual for me.
It was a baptism of sorts back into the material realm and into my
body. I want to continue to reclaim my personal dance of matter –
bearing witness to God in my bones. I want to see this body as an
instrument of worship, which sounds so lofty, until I add that I want
the worship to include play, work, sex, bearing and nursing children,
baking bread, playing the piano, picking weeds, dancing or moving
in a labyrinth. I want to know the divine in fullness and satiation,
hunger and thirst, exertion and rest, fatigue and energy, movement
and song, breathing and silence. Rather than strip my body of the
pleasure of the senses, I want to embody mysticism in the glory and
muddiness of human flesh. I want to see our bodies as part of the
wild flesh of the world. And the remarkable truth is that the ways
you use your body or that your body speaks can be an entrance to the
divine. Thomas Moore says that "the move downward into the body
is also a movement toward soul."[38]

As the city warms and the humidity increases, I feel the Mystery in
the occasional and gentle breeze that brushes over my skin as I walk to
the subway, in the feel of water weighing down my hair after a luke-
warm shower, the prickle of bark on my back as I lean against the syca-
mores in the park, and in rain droplets that course over my face during
an afternoon storm. My children, I can tell, are so much more adept
at this – so much closer to this way of knowing the divine. They glory
in touch and trying to move their tongues to create new sounds. Their
bodies are one of their primary ways of perceiving the world right now,
and of knowing. Today I want to learn from them and reclaim this
deep bodily knowing – to gather my own matter back into the realm
of the sacred (where it has always abided though at times unbeknown
to me). I fetch my limbs, my breath, my vision and heartbeats from
wherever they have been flung. This gathering is today's prayer.

I look at each part of my body, *thou,* and reteach loveliness. If we
allow matter to carry the dust of divinity, then we carry the same.
Galway Kinnell has a poem, "Saint Francis and the Sow" that I read
during three months of bed rest with my first son, Jude. Simply put,

my body has a hard time holding babies in. I'm not sure why. I can get pregnant easily enough, but my body wants to give birth too early – way too early. When I was pregnant with my first I didn't yet know this, and my son was almost born at 26 weeks. I felt so responsible for this aberration in my body's mechanisms. I felt so angry at the precious thou that is my body and myself. And in that terrain, a dear friend sent me the Kinnell poem and I memorized this portion of it, until its truth began to take hold.

> *The bud*
> *stands for all things,*
> *even for those things that don't flower,*
> *for everything flowers, from within, of self-blessing;*
> *though sometimes it is necessary*
> *to reteach a thing its loveliness,*
> *to put a hand on its brow*
> *of the flower*
> *and retell it in words and in touch*
> *it is lovely*
> *until it flowers again from within, of self-blessing.*

— Excerpt from "Saint Francis and the Sow"

It's tempting to behold the micro-geography of the body's aberrations, rejections, diseases, traumas and oppressions in the same way I see the city. They are not the easiest way for me to touch the sacred. But a healthy mysticism requires that we confront matter here too. If we are going to dance with the Mystery through our bodies when they move gracefully and beautifully, we have to stay with them in their pain and suffering and losses, knowing that God meets us there too. Because mysticism does not and should not transcend the body, we must enter into the oppression – sexism, racism, abuse, gender identity, chronic pain – wherever our wounds lay.

In my three-month bed rest, I had to coax my body to accept the love I had never shown. I tried to begin to believe that my skin and bones and frame and shadowed places within were an entrance to the sacred, difficult as that was to bear when they weren't working the way I wanted them to.

When I think of prayer, my first association is with spoken words since this is what prayer meant as a child. That has changed through the years, but the latest iteration is in learning how to root prayer in the body that is then rooted to earth – these two precious intermediaries of the divine. Our bodies are our very presence in the world and without our bodies there would be no possibility of experience, of knowing the sensate world.[39] Without our bodies, I am less and less sure how, if at all, we would know God or have a direct experience with the divine. Our bodies allow us the opportunity to know the Mystery in a way that is unmediated by hierarches or authorities. Perhaps it is because I am pulled earthward so much more these days, but if I cannot enter into prayer through my body, I simply cannot pray. If I cannot find God in the flesh and blood, I cannot find God. I have needed to find God in the practicalities of skin and sweat and milk because I have chosen to have a child, not just once, but twice.

Second Child

You did not know that he would
stretch you wide and long as roped
soap bubbles in butterflied wind.

You did not know the weight
from within of his body pressing
your heart's bruised cavities.

You did not know his cells
would swim in you forever,
collect at sites of illness, heal.

Today he drapes over you like
sheets wet with dew. The knife
is in his iris—charcoal, hunger,

innocence—in what you cannot
give, wounded by birth, sore
in every dark place, and pulled

earthward. This you chose, again.

One of the ways that our human bodies (and the body of the earth, for that matter) are invitations into the mystical is by their calendrical and cyclical nature. For example, in the solar rhythm of winter, I am brought within, to a place of deeper listening, of hunkering down, of sitting by the fire. In the solar rhythm of spring, I begin again, cultivate hope, and try, like Mary Oliver says in her poem "Spring" to forgive the past for everything. Summer is a physical time where we abide in our bodies – we wear fewer clothes, we dive into waters, we lay in the sun, we move. In autumn, we know the bounty of harvest, we gather around a table and share what has been given and we prepare our hearts for the cold, hopefully sharing the table with those we love. Of course, there are times that the solar-based seasons are not in line with our souls, but there is still an invitation of each season that feeds and nurtures mystics and non-mystics alike.

There are also lunar rhythms – the moon waxing and waning and shining and hiding and beckoning us to do the same. And there is the associated rhythm of ocean tides to the moon, even for those of us who are landlocked. In the daily Ashtanga yoga practice, the days of full and new moon are considered days of rest – recognizing that our bodies and souls are affected by the cycles of the moon and that moving with either too much or too little energy could harm us. These movements and cycles and how they touch and affect us if we can let them are all ways of prayer, invitations toward mysticism, unity and participation in these grand cycles.

Symeon the Theologian said "we awaken as the Beloved in every last part of our body."[40] God, then, is not only in the solar and lunar rhythms and all they awaken in us, but also is in the feminine rhythms of ovulation and shedding, of pregnancy and labor, of filling and emptying, of life and of death, of breath in and breath out, of worry and peace, of desire and abstinence. Beverly Lanzetta says that, "Every day, women write the body of divinity through the text of their bodies."[41] And though I am not an expert on the male body, I know that God, then, is in masculine rhythms as well – subtle and long-arced as they are.

Women and men are reawakening to the beauty, suffering, rhythms and cycles of their own and other's bodies and this awareness will only serve to help us write the body of divinity. When I was coming of age, there was no available wisdom on the rhythms (an inherent wisdom) of a woman's ovulation cycle. There was no way to crack the code of my body. Thankfully that has changed and now women have access to understanding the old wisdom of our bodies. Many women these days are exploring the ways their bodies change in just one ovulation cycle as well as over the cycle of their lives. There are four seasons to each cycle wherein our hormones shift and with them, so does our experience of the world. There are four invitations to a different way of being that intersects with and nurtures mystical connection.

The first few days of a woman's cycle (historically understood as a moon cycle due to its length and the way that a woman's cycle lines up with the phases of the moon if she lives outside) is menstruation, which is also considered akin to winter. It is a time that our pace is slowed, we crave quiet and our gaze is more internal. While the lengths of each phase can vary, depending on the woman and her season of life, the next phase is spring or pre-ovulation – when our energy lifts and we are creative and playful, able to begin new things and start again. Then comes ovulation or summer. This is a sensual and sexual time – a time of nurturing; the gaze is often outward. The last days of the cycle are the luteal phase, the internal autumn. I wonder how different my experience of my body would have been when I came of age had I not seen this autumnal phase as pathological (think of all the negative associations of PMS). What if I knew this season for what it is – the time to prepare for the winter to come. This last autumnal phase is a time of hunger, a time where we are on edge, where we tell the truth and are enthralled with ideas and knowledge.

The liturgies of the earth and animal bodies go on and on. These are just a few of the liturgies of matter, just as sacred and profound as the liturgies of any church or religion. I want to memorize them as I would a creed, so that they can bless and carry me when I need them to.

I tend to be hard on my body. I demand too much. I push too

hard. I ignore pain. I am beginning to see how this very thing that I have considered a strength is crowding out the sacred. When I'm in the winter or menstruation season of my cycle, I tend to demand the same "performance" of myself and my body as any other time. And in the end, I just fall flat on my face. These muddy areas of my own weakness or need are so challenging to honor. I want to fight back. I want to be okay. I want to be strong. I don't want to have to go on bed rest with every pregnancy. But what if I could stop fighting and surrender to my own need, my own rhythms, my own body? What if I could find a connection with the divine via my own vulnerability?

Inherent in these vulnerabilities and rhythms is our sexuality. Many men and women (myself included) have relegated their sexuality to side alleys of shame or hedonism sometimes due to abuse, addiction, trauma and sometimes due to the ways that women's bodies (especially) are labeled as profane for their seductive powers. But I am trying to experience God as deep within my earthbound body and sexuality is another, albeit daunting, landscape for reclamation. A fully developed sexuality needs to be welcomed into my idea of divinity. Some traditions are much further along this path than I am, having been raised in the tradition of Eve.

If I include my sexuality as an invitation to know and experience the divine, it will also require that I descend to the wounds and trauma that are woven together with my sexuality. Muddy mysticism, it seems, nearly requires that any violence done to the body/soul be attended to and witnessed. This is the long, slow work of healing. It is sometimes tempting to imagine that moving toward the Mystery can mean leaving our wounds behind, though I have not found that to be true. The Mystery demands our whole person – pained and all: the ugly, the beautiful and the quotidian details in between. Wherever we have been burned, we have to traverse that scorched landscape and move back through the ashes, until we find a meadow.

Birth of a Meadow

Flame to forest, a death—
I do not abandon this sacrament

though I clear coal-jeweled
bark, felled trees, push

boulders back to the edge.
Hands cradle crisp bodies

of wrens, charred ponderosa
limbs. Ash smudges over mine.

This is work that draws blood.
This, my sacrifice, on altars of soil.

*

I wait for baptismal rains—
edged, weary, masked black.

This plot of land cleared
and bare resembles a burial

ground. But the soil harbors
clover seeds that will nakedly

search for sky, coveted by hands
of wind. Meadow flower,

you will push through. I do not
abandon life. Rain, wash me clean.

It can be terrifying to be a body, maybe especially as a woman, given how much violence the female body has been subjected to and the unruly power of giving birth. And I know that as a white woman, I can't even begin to understand how terrifying it can be to be a female body with a different color skin. But I experience that we are not alone in that vulnerability – that God is vulnerable in our bodies as well. In *Becoming Animal: An Earthly Cosmology*, David Abram says:

Corporeal life is indeed difficult. To identify with the sheer physicality of one's flesh may seem lunatic. The body is an imperfect and breakable entity vulnerable to a thousand and one insults – to scars and the scorn of others, to disease, decay, and death. Small wonder, then, that we prefer to abstract ourselves whenever we can, imagining ourselves into theoretical spaces less fraught with insecurity, conjuring dimensions more amenable to calculation and control... Thus do we shelter ourselves from the harrowing vulnerability of bodied existence. But by the same gesture we also insulate ourselves from the deepest wellsprings of joy.

I think of my own harrowing physical vulnerabilities – my body going into labor early, the dilapidated hospital, the way that the doctor's questions sliced through my heart like a knife – *Would you like us to try to resuscitate your child when he is born?* I remember running down the hallway in nothing but a hospital gown screaming for Aaron when they separated us because there were no private rooms available. God was at risk there, too, in my body. And in my son's body, tucked inside of mine, his heart wanting to beat strong and true and long. These bodies are the dwelling places of the sacred, as is the body of the earth. But neither are gentle, invulnerable places.

Vessel

Human desire is the very image of God within us.

— Thomas Traherne

Aaron and I are back in the throes of unknowing since we lost the Quaker Bridge Road house. We are looking for new jobs (again). After the boys are in bed, most nights, we look through new job postings. Aaron goes through the postings first, circling the ones that fit his areas of specialty and expertise. I go through next, crossing out the ones that are located in places that I can't imagine calling home. I hate being the one that crosses out rather than circles. I hate how we have done this for so many years now and still to no avail. There is heaviness in the air tonight and we keep our words sparse. The thin newspaper rustles like leaves. The scratch of his pen on the paper brings me anxiety. I don't want to keep saying no. When will I be able to give a full-hearted yes? In the background, we hear the deep breaths of our two sons, sleeping soundly, trusting us to know whether we should stay or go and where.

Aaron circles a job possibility in Phoenix, Arizona, where we lived previously for four years while he was getting his PhD. A few minutes later, he hands me the page and I look down at his blue pen marks. The very name of the city causes my body to tense. I feel slammed by a wall of desert heat, depressed by the lack of water, the sprawl of suburbia. Everything in my body screams "no."

Sometimes the body has a prophetic imagination. And in my case, it was begging to be included in this discernment process – a portal to a mystical way of knowing. I think of David Abrams when he said, "Our animal senses are neither deceptive nor untrustworthy; they are our access to the cosmos. Bodily perception provides our most intimate entry into a primary order of reality that can be disparaged or dismissed only at our peril." [42]

But despite the peril, almost immediately, I begin arguing within myself. I am so accustomed to a top-down processing and cannot easily submit to a bottom-up processing that allows my body room to speak and even speak first. My mind says that we both have extended family there, people we fiercely love. Other people can make it work and even thrive. Aaron's specialties match up nearly exactly with what the position requires. I learned to survive the desert once.

I ask for a few days to think it over. It is too quiet between us until another car alarm goes off in front of our house. It will probably go off for hours, its owner tucked into an apartment however many blocks away. People have to park wherever remaining spots are available. The car alarm feels like my body shouting in alarm with no one close enough to listen.

As the days pass, my mind continually tries to override my body, making arguments for once again living near family, for Aaron's vocational fulfillment, for being in the beloved West again. All of that is true. I start looking at real estate in Phoenix, trying to imagine what it would be like to move my family there. A few times I can almost picture it. But then I remember the way my body initially reacted so viscerally. What should I do with the deep instinctual knowing? What would it mean to turn a blind eye to the voice of my body, the voice of matter?

For years, I have prayed and pleaded for my instincts to be healed – so that I could process the world from the seat of my body, so that I could experience my body's interior. [43] I left those instincts behind in childhood, like many of us do, and perhaps I more than most. The body's integral components of instinct and desire have been undervalued and unconsciously relegated from our understanding of mysticism. Furthermore, instinctual ways of knowing have often been damaged through trauma, lack of value, and misguided theology.

I was easily convinced through theology and experience that my body was evil and needed to be transcended. Traces of this line of thinking are pervasive in many mystical texts. Most late medieval and post-Reformation mystics in the Christian tradition were proponents of physical asceticism. Asceticism has a patriarchal thread running through it in that it presumes that we have to put our bodies under the subjugation of our minds. And, right or wrong, the body is associated with the realm of the feminine whereas rationality is associated with the realm of the masculine. Furthermore, physical mistreatment of the body was thought to facilitate union with the divine. But there was also an undercurrent in this focus on physical asceticism that one needed inner freedom from the flesh in order to unify with the divine. This line of thinking is something I have to work hard against, both in myself and as I enter the larger conversation of mysticism.

Studies of the Dark

i.

Here is the bitter road that parses
the past from the road of ripened figs.

You used to sacrifice hunger
for vision, sleep for God.

The old way is hard

but you forced sight, and power
is gravity, even in the form
of asceticism.

Wasps sacrifice wings to lay eggs
inside figs. What is more,
they sacrifice flight.

But why did you cut back branches
blazing with fruit?

ii.

Dust off inverted flowers.
Turn the fig inside out.

Take and eat

petals encased in skin,
invisible digested wasps—
pollinators, matchmakers.

This may be your only consolation
when you think of the impasse
God is.

You used to walk the sparse road
of denial turned death.

You used to hold your hands inside out—
emptied.

But that is nearly impossible
now

with figs soft and ready to wither
within the noon hour.

Your hands are full, smeared
with seeds, wasps, petals, juice.

iii.

> *The old way is hard to leave behind.*
> *What takes the place of hunger?*

iv.

> *Gather rocks.*
>
> *Bang them together*
> *to see what sparks fly*
> *from this sort of prayer.*
>
> *Discard mica for siltstone—*
> > *Sometimes life from death*
> > *is indistinguishable.*
>
> *Discard sandstone for basalt—*
> > *Sometimes starvation*
> > *from mysticism.*
>
> *Cicada songs lace through late summer,*
> *steal through your ripened chest,*
> *fray out your back.*
>
> *Follow the long road that sorts out*
> *quartz from hunger, figs from sight.*

As I follow the long road, I come to know that there are so many ways of knowing and this bodily knowing is only one of them. But it is an important one. What do I gain from ignoring my physical instincts? What do I gain from returning to a desert, a place asceticism was born? One definition of mysticism is the pursuit of community with God through instinct or insight. I have the opportunity to abide within the body's peace or to turn against it. Habit asks that I turn against it. But *today* asks that I pay close attention before doing so. And perhaps muddy mysticism asks that I allow my body to be a vessel of the sacred, to be the answer to this one question, banging rocks together, watching sparks fly.

Flesh

*If this body is my very presence in the world, if it is the body that
alone enables me to enter into relations with other presences, if
without these eyes, this voice, or these hands I would be unable
to see, to taste, and to touch things, or to be touched by them – if
without this body, in other words, there would be no possibility of
experience – then the body itself is the true subject of experience.*

— David Abram [44]

We cannot venture into the realm of the body without feeling the
brush of the feminine, if only because the feminine has historically
been more closely associated with the body, for good and ill, and I
have historically associated femininity with my body. The feminine,
at least in an archetypal context, is embodied (or instinctual). It is
the work of mysticism to heal both the masculine and feminine in
oneself and perhaps to heal the images of the masculine and feminine
in God. Thomas Merton says in his "Hagia Sophia" poem: "We do
not see the Blinding One in black emptiness. He speaks to us gently
in ten thousand things, in which His light is one fullness and One
wisdom. I picture God then as light or sun. Less body – more spirit.
The burning. And Mother God is the bush." This perspective is a
common one and one I am familiar with.

The feminine face of God brings me back to the earth, into matter,
into my own breathing body to hear the voice that says, "No, do not
move to Phoenix. Not again. Once was enough." She beckons me
into the liturgy of staying in my skin and learning to recognize the
voice of the body. She beckons me to listen. Due to my ingrained
ascetic strand, I have needed Someone to speak into this, to say *"Lis-
ten!"* in the throes of hunger or longing or fear.

This listening was an especially difficult task after struggling with disordered eating for many years where I betrayed my body's natural instincts. While the disordered eating was initially a result of deep depression and an attempt to *disembody* or escape my body entirely, it later became a twisted (and out of control) ascetic practice. To start with, I viewed the body as peripheral, something to be denied, an *it*, other. But more than that, I wanted a way to make real in the world how small I was becoming. This long act of perpetual hunger was not prayer. It was not healthy fasting but was a turning away from the sacred, from life.

After months of extreme starvation, I touched the corner of Death's robes. On one particular night, I blacked out again. Usually when this would happen, my head would soon clear and light would rush back in assuring me, whether I liked it or not, that I was alive. But this night, alone in my childhood bedroom, it went further. In that dim space of loss of consiousness, I was, for what felt like a moment, still "living" but more disembodied than I had ever been. I felt like I was pure spirit, separating from body, beginning a narrow flight of disentanglement.

I will never know if hearing too many stories about being in between life and death influenced me in the next moments or not, but I felt like I had a decision to make. Would I disentangle entirely from my body, which was by then "back" in the yellow-walled bedroom, lying lifeless and thin and pitifully disregarded on the antique brass bed that had once belonged to my parents? This would be a natural progression on the path I had forged. I had been successful at disappearing in so many realms that completing the path toward disembodiment had some sick integrity. Or would I choose life and seek to push back against that inclination to disappear? Would I take up space literally and figuratively? Would I step back into the conversation of instinct and desire – the origins of which are holy even if the ways in which we enact those desires sometimes are not.

Somewhere in that liminal space which I imagine to be between this world and the beyond, I took a step toward life, back toward earth. I wish I could say that it was because I valued my life for its own sake, because I could say a hearty yes. But there was nothing hearty about those days. I wish that I had been ready to push back against my proclivity toward disappearance and compliance. But that would come later. Closer to the truth at that moment was that I did not want to cause tremendous pain to my family. So I turned toward my weakening body. I woke up to the world, in the middle of the night, and dragged myself into the pitch-black kitchen. And I ate by the yellow glow of the open freezer.

The first bite I took was itself a middle-of-the-night prayer, though I cannot recall what it was. But it was the first bite in a long time that I did not take begrudgingly – that I was able to accept as nourishment. I ate real food that night, but it was the intersection of matter and spirit – of accepting nourishment along with the actual substantive food – that really sustained me.

It was mystical, standing there at the refrigerator, the house dark but for the eerie light of appliances. The forest beyond the house was even darker. And a voice spoke in the darkness, "Take. Eat. This is my body, broken for you." *Broken like you.* "Do this in remembrance of me."

Some might call that sacrilege. But it was the truest form of communion I have yet to partake in. The symbol of the Christian Eucharist infused with matter. A life-giving sacrament. I feel these memories in my body almost like an aura after a migraine. I feel the singe of my own skeleton poking through my skin. I feel the consciousness that can linger patiently outside of the body. I feel the ascent, then the descent, the way my heart pounded as I opened the freezer.

I think I ate ice cream.

> *Within the pulse of flesh,*
> *in the dust of being, where we trudge,*
> *turning our hungry gaze this way and that,*
> *the wings of morning*
> *brush through our blood*
> *as cloud-shadows brush the land.*
> *What we desire travels with us.*
> *We must breathe time as fishes breath water.*
> *God's flight circles us.*
>
> — Denise Levertov [45]

Very, very slowly over the next few years and decades, I learned to welcome the signs of hunger as a rightful voice and as a voice not disconnected to the divine. Still to this day, hunger is part of my sacred liturgy and my spiritual practice. This is one simple entrance into mysticism. Here I circle back, time and again, to be with the Real. I listen to a voice deep within for signs of hunger and satiation. I get lost sometimes, but I can begin again each morning, each meal. For some people, this might be second nature. Eating when hungry and ceasing when full might be unconscious and if that is the case, I have some envy, if I'm honest. But mostly I marvel (and bless) how those instincts are still intact. I hope those individuals can relish in the wholeness of this dance between body and soul, making it an occasionally conscious prayer. For myself, for whom the wires crossed long ago, I continue to embark on this daily fundamental act of prayer. Every day I seek to recover and unbury the voice within, responding to it. Eating is an embodied act and I seek such an embodied mysticism that I cannot help but explore the ways that eating is a bringing forth, an ushering in of life. Barbara Brown Taylor says that "if all life is holy, then anything that sustains life has holy dimensions too." [46] I think of my newborns, only minutes old, finding their way through sheer instinct to my breasts. I think of the way mothers wait and worry over their milk coming in. I think of the elation I feel watching my toddler eating a healthy meal. It is holy – all of it.

Intimacy with our food may be a way to be more intimate with the divine given that the spiritual life needs to be rooted in the dirt. Our food and nourishment are most literally rooted in soil. There are so many old practices and contemporary movements that have surfaced in recent years around the sacredness and divinity of food. We hear how, through what we eat, our bodies are tied together with the land and the ever-widening circles that expand from there, due to an ever-more connected world.

Some who have the privilege and the means may try to make those circles smaller so that justice can be advocated on this basic level of sustenance. Eating inevitably steeps us in issues of justice and equality, poverty and waste. Even the fact that only the privileged have the opportunity to eat organically or locally is a huge problem. But this propulsion into the wider world initiated through our need to nourish our bodies also asks the muddy mystic to engage in sacred activism, rather than retreat into a hermitage.

It's not just eating that can be an entrance into mysticism, but making love, hugging a child, planting a seed, making a purchase, talking to a friend, hanging laundry. These are all entrances and also grounds for sacred activism, which is a strand of mysticism. I am trying to choose the ways that open for me and make my life into a prayer.

Symbol

*The names of God lie coiled within the physical forms of things;
our particular and uniquely human task is to spring the trap and
set them free. They cannot manifest apart from the sensible realm
but neither will they manifest automatically within unless there is
a further act of conscious transformation. That is our joy. Working
within the raw materials of the physical world, we are to give
"birthing" and "body" to the names of God so that the invisible
becomes visible. We are midwives of the Spirit.*

— Cynthia Borgeault [47]

It has been the work of my own particular mystical way to explore different names, faces and symbols of God in an effort to salvage the divine for myself. It has been an act of preservation. For many years, God lived in a realm of my disappointment, disillusionment, despair. And as long as I assumed a rather standard definition of divinity (which initially was attached to more typical titles) I remained stuck in these places of desolation. For me, standard definitions of divinity have so many complicated associations with qualities that are inherently inhibitive or exclusionary and were likely designed to be just that. But all names, faces and symbols of the divine have varying associations and can dramatically impact our interactions with the divine as well as break an individual out of binary modalities of thought around the perceived essence of the divine.

Today, I understand – and most certainly misunderstand – God to be outside of the bounds of gender. But I still sometimes use the names of Father and Mother. I also use Sophia and Shekinah, sacred and divine, Near and Far, Real and Mystery to describe the divine and to name what we call God. I have known God as Spirit,

as gloriously transcendent, the God of the sky. I have known God
as Emmanuel, *God with us,* and as Jesus. I have known God as the
deepest voice within. I have known God as the Cloud of Unknowing,
the Holy Mystery, the Living Wind, and as One. I have known God
in a quietly meandering stream and as the Spirit of the Universe. I
have known God as Goddess. I have known or perceived the forest
face of God and now I am trying to learn the city face of God.

Through my work in Armenia, I see the face of God in the shining
faces of people with special needs. Their collective path to joy feels
profound despite all the pain that they have carried. At our New Year
celebrations, I marvel at the ways their bodies move and dance in ec-
stasy. I laugh at how clumsy I am in comparison. And at nearly every
gathering, they sing. A child who recently watched videos of those
we serve and love with reciprocity in Armenia said, "They are always
singing and dancing." That they are.

I have also learned to see the face of God in the many faces of peo-
ple abandoned in the large, cruel psychiatric institutions in Arme-
nia. While this is more difficult experientially, it is perhaps even more
important so that those who are institutionalized are not rejected or
forgotten – so that we do not cease seeking justice and honor on their
behalf. Mirabai Starr says, "Whenever we tend to a single strand, we
are participating in the care of the whole. When we turn our face from
the suffering of any being and walk away, we are exiling ourselves from
the Beloved."[48] Even those who are institutionalized and abandoned,
abused and mistreated, are not simply and solely wounded. They are
not just in pain. A person can be eradicated by their pain and I do
not wish to do them this disservice. They also know the full spectrum
of human emotion. They also know how to dance. They also likely
skipped through puddles as a child. They also sing. Or used to.

I have seen the childlike face of God and the river face of God.
Sometimes it is effortless to see these faces, images and symbols of the
divine around me and sometimes it is painstaking work. But most
definitely God is still unfolding *for me,* and perhaps still unfolding.

As you know by now, the first face of God I knew was the Father

God associated with Evangelical Protestantism within Christianity. I knew Him when I would sit on a sacred rock I discovered in the quiet forests of Northern Arizona. He was both loving and fierce, both merciful and demanding. Whether from the tendrils of my own soul or theology (and probably both), so many of my experiences of God and Jesus were ridden with guilt and attached to a conviction that I was deeply flawed and sinful. Stuck within this paradigm, I often could not see how I could ever be redeemed or valued. This view of the divine exacerbated my perfectionist tendencies and drove me so far into the ground, so far into an act of disappearance that culminated in severely disordered eating. There I was pressed hard on all sides by the earth until I had to let go. I had to be dust. I had to be weak and small and powerless to even try to be perfect. And what a gift that ultimately was.

It took giving up completely on God for God to come to me again. It took bearing a sense of abandonment, a belief that God left me, to find something new and to let the old unravel. I have known the slow and arduous work of decay. I have also come to know that as things decay, they can bring their equivalents into being, if we can open our hearts wide enough, which is easier said than done. [49] I wonder sometimes if Father God, the God of my youth, did in fact leave me in terms of consolation and solace so that something else could take root and grow within.

In my early twenties, when I was living in Los Angeles, I began meeting with my first spiritual director, a practice I still continue to this day. I had never heard of spiritual direction until a friend mentioned that I might find it helpful. He knew that I was no longer part of a church or spiritual community but that my longing for the Mystery was the central longing in my life. He could see that I was hungry for companionship and that I was trying to build a new spiritual home.

Though today there are spiritual directors within and without of nearly every tradition, at that time it was a more exclusively Catholic practice, at least in the United States. Spiritual direction within the Catholic tradition goes back to the 4th century and is a widespread practice. The director's role is not to convert people or influence their theology, as I understand it. Their role is to be with people as they explore and deepen their relationship with the divine. It is simple, really. It is not therapy or intellectual conversation. It is not even guidance as much as it is listening, asking questions and waiting. At my friend's urging, I went to the Catholic Diocese of Los Angeles and met with a nun for about an hour. I told her who I was, and how I experienced and didn't experience God. She said that she thought she had just the right person for me. She wrote a name and number on a small piece of paper and I called Mary Ellen the next day.

Mary Ellen and I started meeting together right away. Our time together was slow and meditative. We met in a small room in her home about once a month. We held silence together and spoke of the larger Silence within which I lived. I spoke with her about how my heart pushed back hard and fiercely against many of the central doctrines with which I was raised. They offended me, plain and simple. Finally, one day, after hearing me go on and on about this for many months she asked, quietly, if it was possible that what I thought of as my own heart or voice was the voice of God within me. She asked, only, if this was possible. The truth is that it sounded completely and terrifyingly heretical.

My reaction is not uncommon for those raised in Evangelicalism. A beloved friend raised in the same tradition as I, who walked blessedly closely to me through my own unraveling and eating disorder, wrote to me recently that she continues to be struck by people who trust their inner moral compass to guide them – people who hold to their own principals in thoughtful and powerful ways. We were specifically talking about André and Magda Trocmé. André was a pastor in the French village of Le Chambon and he and Magda (along with the support of the whole village) subversively protected and saved the lives of many Jews during the Holocaust. My friend said that it is healing for her to hear stories about people who trust themselves (when it goes against the theology or religious authority of the time) and then do beautiful things in the world. She said that growing up she felt like she should fundamentally not trust herself but that she should always look to the Bible to inform her thoughts and beliefs. She then spoke to the tension, confusion and sometimes crippling anxiety when her intuitive knowing did not line up with what the Bible seemed to say she should believe.

I knew exactly what she meant. And I immediately remembered what my spiritual director had asked me. *Was it possible that what I thought of as my own heart or voice was actually the voice of God within me?* I wanted what she said to be true, but I quickly assumed that if this was true, that if I allowed the possibility of God within me, I would lose God through the contamination of my own body and self. And while I wasn't able to accept this possibility and her words at that time, she planted a seed deep within me and there it awaited the right time to germinate. Later I was able to begin to push back against that which offended me, even if with great fear initially. And today, I can answer with a resounding yes. Yes, that is possible. And thank goodness.

Now that I have birthed two babies and beheld them in such glorious innocence, my reaction those many years ago disturbs and offends me. The fact that I assigned my own being so much shame breaks my heart. I lost so much of the divine through this wrong appropriation of shame. I lost so much of the Real because of my disdain for the body. Now I know that prayer (existence) needs a body; it needs to be rooted. God has many faces, many bodies, *one of them mine.* Nowadays, I can listen to that still and deep voice within, though it took years (and years) to clear away some of the debris that was blocking my ear canals.

This body was ravaged a few times and in a few different ways, but it is still a sanctuary.

In the following years, the divine took on the face of the Holy Mystery or Sophia – lovely, encompassing, set apart, wise, infused into each and every layer, albeit somewhat distant. I could not fathom or believe that Sophia cared about the particulars of my life or the world, because She is so unknown and removed from earthly life. But she also planted seeds into the hidden soils of my heart around the darkness of God. Thomas Merton speaks of this aspect of the divine in his "Hagia Sophia" poem: "Perhaps in a certain very primitive aspect Sophia is the unknown, the dark, the nameless Ousia. Perhaps she is even the Divine Nature... And perhaps she is in infinite light unmanifest, not even wanting to be known as Light." It was a profound shift for me to fathom that the divine may not want to be known as light; the associations from my childhood were so strong. But in the lostness and confusion of walking an unknown path at midnight, this was a solace of sorts. In my places of defeat and loneliness, I dove toward this unknown and landed in the lap of the Black Madonna, where I still am sitting, quiet and in awe.

The history of the Black Madonna is complex, religiously and racially. I have realized with growing sorrow and grief that I learned about the Black Madonna in her appropriated form without even realizing it. Ironically, as I moved away from a male white God and into more alternative and feminine faces of God, I was still unable to escape the reaches of patriarchy and white supremacy. The history of white people appropriating the spirituality of people of color is undeniable and problematic, to the extent that I have wondered if I should even include my perception of the Black Madonna at all. People of color have been denied access to the divine using some of the same strategies that have been used with women. Tragically, due to the widespread oppression that black people specifically have experienced, we do not have access to many of their mystical texts. Sometimes we may have access to them, but do not even realize that they have been appropriated or unacknowledged.

The *Mystic Soul Project* is one example of the resurgence and protection of these voices in the United States. Teresa P. Mateus claims the mission of the *Mystic Soul Project* as activism, mysticism and healing centered around the life experiences of people of color. They create space for conversations, relationship-building, practices and other programming centered around the experience of people of

culture and work to reclaim ancestral practices that have been aban-
doned or erased by Western traditions. When the *Mystic Soul Project*
speaks, I move aside. And I listen.

Complicated as it is, I was introduced to the Black Madonna
through Jungian scholars who interpret the Black Madonna primar-
ily through the lens of Catholicism. I have since learned that nowa-
days the Black Madonna lies at the crossroads of pagan and Christian
belief systems. At one point, she was pre-Christian. In her Christian
iteration, she is associated with the Virgin Mary.

There are conflicting opinions about the origin and nature of her
dark skin. To Jungians, the literal darkness of the statues speaks to the
shadow side of a virginal figure; she is associated with the primordial
feminine. Some legends subsequently ascribe her blackness due to
aging or smoke from candles or fires. But to me she is much more
than a statue that has been charred. And furthermore, it is arguable
that she is not solely a psychological symbol of the darker mother
of Christ, but rather originally a statue of the Black Goddess or the
Great Mother of Africa and Egypt and that the story of her being
charred was an attempt to subvert her true nature. [50]

When I learned this, when I saw how easily the voices of those on
the margins are erased, and when I saw how even this marginalization
was embedded in my own journey of trying to stop marginalizing
women's mystical voices, I was deeply troubled at the irony. While I
am captivated and taken with her, her original followers have been
erased from her public story.

To make it more complicated, while I have no firsthand experience
with being oppressed because of my skin color, I do have firsthand
experience being on the side of the oppressor and carry the innate
sense of proper guilt that comes from that history. My family once
enslaved people in Georgia, and not that long ago. And as I learn
more about systemic racism, I see that all white people including
my family continue to this day to benefit from enslaved human be-
ings and the ongoing societal structures that oppress and degrade.
Not only do we benefit, but we must be held accountable for our

ancestor's crimes. And we must be as honest as we can possibly be.

With all this in mind, I continue to wrestle with whether it is right to claim the Black Madonna as a transformative symbol for me. But as I have tried to find a way to wiggle out of including her, I realize that while I cannot claim her, she claimed me and the hold she has on my heart is irrevocable. She demands that I right some of the wrongs – that I be accountable for the ways she was appropriated – and that I speak of what I have learned. She has not only urged me to examine all symbols and ideas more carefully and through the lens of oppression, but she also invites me into a space of belonging and transformation.

The Black Madonna embodies the problem of associating darkness with what the world does not value. Even in her colonized form, she represents what the authorities of Christianity have rejected. She is a spiritual mirror of what we have done in our society. *And* she is also the one who first allowed me to re-imagine darkness in spirituality as holy, regenerative and as the source of new life. She is one who urged me to tend and re-sacralize that which lay beyond the spiritual-ly-approved boundaries. She led me into those murky places where I found a flourishing and earth-bound mysticism. I hope the Great Mother of Egypt would be proud.

The version of the Virgin Mary that I knew from the tradition in which I was raised did not capture me the way the Black Madon-na did. She was too nice. Too white. Too perfect. When the Black Madonna found me, I was able to slowly but surely begin the work of disentangling myself from the fears of offending some version of God that was exacting and relentless, in whom I no longer believed, but who still haunted the outskirts of my soul. I was able to value, articulate and abide in the mysticism of the dark.

As often happens, when something changes in your soul, you start seeing signs all over of what to you is profoundly new. After staying away from church for nearly ten years, I recently found myself at an Episcopal Church in New York City at odd hours, staring at a paint-ing of the Black Madonna in one of the side chapels. I have uncov-ered in books and in conversation others who know her and love her and also are seated in her bountiful lap. She does not want to simply include me (or any of us) in her way of being. I think she wants us to belong. She wants us to find a home in our own lives, and in her. And as I understand, she cares most about doing that for those on the margins. She never asks me to retreat from my life to be with her, for she is a Mother. She knows. Instead, she asks me only and always to stay in my own life, to get dirty and wet with my kids when they are playing in puddles after a rain storm, to embrace the every day.

It is not lost on me that it was not until I became a mother that I could finally begin to pray and love and be held by a feminine aspect of the divine. I'm not sure if that is a common experience or not. But what I imagine is common is that a change in identity of any kind precipitates a change in how one relates to the divine.

I became a mother for the first time in 2003 when I was 24 years old, living and working in the small mountain town of Kapan, Armenia. I was a Peace Corps volunteer, working at an orphanage with a significant number of abandoned children and young adults with special needs. It was here that my heart broke open to create space for these individuals. Like a fig split open, all my petals, and all of my flowering parts, all of my fruit, were vulnerable to the sky. What happened there was irrevocable. It led Aaron and I to attempt to adopt one young woman. When that failed due to immigration and adoption laws in both Armenia and the United States and when I learned that she and the others would live out their days in a psychiatric institution, it led me down winding roads in winter, traversing mountain paths with only my own fears for company. I did not want her (and the others, whom I also already loved, hook, line and sinker) to be imminently institutionalized. I had been to those institutions. I knew their desperation, cruelty, neglect and abuse. I wanted to bring them to a home (something I still ironically have not been able to do for myself).

Your Journey Home

– for Bridget, who was there

When the driver saw us, he cursed, mumbled,
but let us climb slowly into his rumbling bus.
We filled those kilometers with sea-sickness,

mountain-sickness, home-sickness. Bag after
bag of bile and loss I chucked out the window,
littering switchbacks with disregard and hope.

Three trucks overturned on icy mountain passes
that day. One man's face smeared with blood.
We held your lives in our twenty-something hands.

This kind of trust is not something we earned.
Speaking your language like seven-year-olds
we bribed, dared, fought, stared back hard.

We scrapped together kindness. My mind cast
out far over frozen Lake Sevan, skimmed
the surface and was reeled back in by the driver

who caught my eye in his rearview mirror
as I blinked quickly, built a dam. His curses
switch-backed into kindness I never expected.

After you were settled, I came outside with my rag
heart, a bucket full of water, soap and an extra
handful of dram to pay for the damages.

He shooed me away after blessing my sagging
shoulders, after wiping down my stench-streaked
jacket when all I had asked for was that he drive

you safely home.

*

After you were sleeping on floor-bound
mattresses, tucked between second-hand
sheets with peonies, cradling the quiet,
cradling stuffed bears, I left you, looking
back, fighting back, tethered and bound
to the song of your breath. I left you
with people who did not yet love you
and flew west for thirty hours, wrapped
the planet round my heart and then bled
for ten days like a mother who had just
given birth, sore in every dark place.

They are the children of my heart, though they are fully grown. Loving them has been an initiation into the rising and falling of motherhood. But even this sort of motherhood did not elevate and sacralize the feminine within me. I was mother to them and I could have still been a man and loved them as I did.

Seven years later, I had Jude – the first child of my body. And as a woman becomes a mother again (as if for the first time) with the birth or adoption of each child, I became a mother anew. But this time it was my very body, my very womanhood that allowed this life to be. I could not help but see the beauty and purity and power of being a woman. Though it had been there all along, and would have been there whether or not I had born a child of my own body, I had not been able to see it. Not yet. But in Jude's birth, I was reborn, baptized in my own waters.

Vivienne, my current spiritual director, recently talked about the biblical story of Nicodemus. She said that she didn't know whether spiritual birth is a metaphor for physical birth or vice versa. But it didn't matter to me. I changed as the waters of life mixed with blood when my child was born. I brought forth life and felt the underside of death. This power cauterized old wounds in me.

I have written elsewhere of the welcome reclamation of my own body in this act of bearing, loving and tending children. As I wash them, wipe them down, clean their noses and ears, take food from my mouth to place in theirs, nurture them with my milk, the shame that I wrapped around my own body is undone, one tight stitch at a time. And the Black Madonna has held my hand through this, for she loves this body of mine. She loves bodies. And she loves the world – not in some grandiose or salvific way, but she loves the world for itself.

The Black Madonna beckons a deepening shift in me from Light to Dark, Day to Night, from Sun to Moon, from Logos to Eros, from Spirit to Matter, from the archetypal Masculine to Feminine. I know that each infuses meaning and vitality into the other, and that we need opposing principles, but until now I have given over my life to the Sun, the Logos, Spirit. I was raised with an exclusively white male God. God was the "head" of the "body" of Christ. A man, similarly, was head of his home. Only men were leaders in the churches where I was raised. And as a pendulum must swing, so I swing. Honestly, I was not even conscious of the dearth in my identity until now. If this old perspective were true, God is apart from me – other and male.

Long ago, when Mary Ellen suggested that I listen to the voice deep within about matters of theology, I was terrified. How could a God so other make His voice heard in me? It wasn't until I recognized the scars of patriarchy for what they are and realized the schism in me that came from undervaluing my femininity – that I began to explore these more feminine faces of God, and other alternate faces and symbols.

The world needs this reclamation of feminine images of the divine (and it is most certainly underway). We need them to be pervasive and integrated into our daily lives, our worship, our sacred activism. Jungian psychologist and author Fred Gustafson says of the Black Madonna, "Never before in history have we so sorely needed to re-connect ourselves with Her mysteries, to revere Her giving and taking and to learn again that there is no spiritual life of any worth that is not rooted in soil." [51]

Today I agree wholeheartedly. But the feminine symbols and faces of God were initially a struggle for me to approach. Her language and ways were so foreign that even when I was drawn to Her, there was not an entrance. For many years, I was disturbed by this conversation of gender as it relates to God. It was too political and too much of a land mine, perhaps simply because I had yet to value the feminine as much as the masculine. The predominant culture had overridden my own sense of value.

I do wonder if one day we will move completely beyond gendered images of the sacred. Perhaps full initiation sees both the underworld and the upperworld as equally masculine and feminine or neither. [52] I hear Rebecca Solnit's voice when she says,

If the genders were not opposite but a spectrum of variations on some central theme of being human, if there were many ways to execute your role or refuse it, and liberation for each gender was seen as being allowed to take up what had been considered the proper role and goods and even feelings of the other or find some third (or seventh) way, then the citadel would be broken and everyone could travel freely. [53]

I imagine that even then God could travel more freely.

The Black Madonna integrates that which is unilluminated into my ideas of the feminine and the divine. She dismantles my inclination and training to always reach for what is illuminated, and what has frankly failed me in this season. She is embodied. She is blessedly muddy and dark. She is the tree of life. Hers is the body of the earthbound sycamore outside my window as it extends arms up to the heavens, and digs roots ever deeper into the earth.

She is close to the cycles of life – birth, death, and resurrection. The Black Madonna is not simply the virginal or even the archetypal mother surrounded by a great light. Neither is she overly sexualized. But she is more whole – more earthy, sensual, passionate, fiery, robust, connected, soft, and engaging. She is in touch with her own desires, as I long to be, and does not measure these in terms of sacred or profane. She loves the dance of spirit and matter.

There are other profound sides to the Black Madonna that have converged to make her such a powerful symbol. Her statues have long been pilgrimage sites for those in need of healing, for those who suffer or are afflicted, for those who are oppressed or marginalized. She is also the patron saint of abandoned daughters who rejoice in their outcast state and can use it to renew the world. [54] While I have loving parents and am far from an abandoned daughter in the literal sense, I know the regeneration that can (eventually) come from being on the outside. And I know how hard won it is.

And as I have moved closer to the Black Madonna, I have embraced and elevated the shadows that touch and belong to the divine. For so long, I felt compelled to uphold God as light, as if dark was degrading. This is what I was taught as a child. The racist implications and associations of this training are devastating. If dark is degraded, then there is no protection for blackness, no holiness in darkness, and no protection for black bodies. But I find the Black Madonna to be a powerful antidote to this perspective.

And as I have learned more about the colonization of the Black Madonna, she has demanded something more of me both spiritually and practically. She has opened my eyes into the many problematic layers of my indoctrination – religious and cultural. She demands that I do more than elevate the unilluminated spaces and also simultaneously work to dismantle a society that continues to exploit, colonize, and wound black bodies (and symbols). She is willing to hold and confront desolation. I must be too. She is a healing figure who is intimate with oppression, grief, and my own entanglement with the world. She is comfortable with the starless regions.

If my own spiritual journey thus far is any indication of how it will continue, I imagine it will meander and circle, much like my journey toward trying to call some place home. I imagine the face and symbols around the divine that I know today will also change with time. I imagine and hope I may not always be here in Queens, either. I hope that as I circle this labyrinth, I will move surely toward the center. I know that I will have to keep going barefoot on this path in order to do so – shedding the layers, shedding the fear, continually coming to a place of bewilderment. Like the poet Maureen Morehead says in her book *In the Yellow Room:*

> *One must take off her fear like clothing.*
> *One must travel at night;*
> *This is the seeking after God.*

At some point, in this experience of seeking, of ascending and descending into the heart of God through new names, symbols, stories and images, all names finally disappear. I am silenced. And God is neither Mother nor Father, neither Dark nor Light, neither Earthly nor Heavenly, Far or Near, Within or Without. And this wordless place is where a muddy mysticism leaves us. There is the naming of God, which is essential on the ascent, and the un-naming (or denial of names) that takes place on the descent. This is the paradox within presence. This is the grate I want to slip through, where I can stop asking the question around what or where and just start living it – between the ruckus and the wild.

Meadow

*[There is] a new breed of religious beings seeking direct experience,
not the lessons of authorities. At the same time, they know for
some reason others have difference experiences, so they do not try to
proclaim their experience as Truth. They may be the first humans
to have to live with a direct spiritual knowledge that is recognized
as fundamentally uncertain.*

— Elaine Aron [55]

The boys were in bed; the lights were dim. I lit a few candles around
our living room and started boiling water for tea on our small stove-
top. Aaron was reading on the couch and I slipped in next to him and
kicked a few toys off the coffee table as I stretched out my legs. He
knew that my initial reaction to moving to Phoenix had been nega-
tive. And he also knew that I had searched my heart (and hundreds of
property ads) to see if it would be possible. I imagine he couldn't help
but hope. I took a deep breath in preparation of speaking and the
whistle on the kettle blessedly postponed our conversation. I hopped
up and nearly sprinted to the kitchen so the shrill whistle wouldn't
awaken the boys. I poured my tea slowly, stirring and steeping and
procrastinating. I took another deep breath and walked into the liv-
ing room. Aaron looked up from his book.

I told him that I didn't think I could move to Phoenix again. I told
him how my body had spoken when I thought of the prospect, how I
had waffled, but that I had landed finally in agreement with the way
my body spoke with such assurance and conviction. I told him about
how I need to withhold my *yes* when the grim spirit of perfectionism,
which expects me to be able to thrive anywhere, presses down on me. I
told him about how I need to withhold my *yes* when the sacrifice seems

too great. I told him that I wanted a place where I could see some stars.

He accepted it with a mixture of grace and frustration. He had already bought the ticket to Phoenix for an interview. He thought out loud that perhaps he would just fly back anyhow, visit with his mom and do the interview just for the experience of it. All of that made me nervous: what if he was offered the job and I had to say no again? But I conceded.

If it's not already obvious, one of the most difficult aspects about living in a city is the way I miss the stars. I have a physical ache for them, the way I ache for my babies' bodies when they are tiny and apart from me. It is the stars that make me think I cannot go to Phoenix or stay here much longer for that matter. When we were driving to my hometown of Flagstaff recently, on a family trip, Jude looked out the car window and said with a mixture of awe and fear, "What are those?"

I looked out and said, "What are what, baby?" He pointed up to the sky with his tiny chubby hands. I said quietly, "Those are stars," while tears ran down my face for the fact that they were foreign to him. It was then that the urgency to leave became physical. And yet we still have not found a way forward. So, we wait. Like we have done so many times before.

Flagstaff is the first Dark Sky City, which means that there are multiple restrictions on how many lights there can be in city limits and of what variety. The goal is to keep the sky clear at night for stargazing. And dark it is. I have never beheld as many stars as in Northern Arizona. The way they sing in the sky is unlike any other place. Living citybound, I can barely remember what their song is like.

It is this longing and ache that I want to escape but I wonder if these can be an entrance into a sacred space.

Last night I dreamt that I was standing in a meadow, in vast open wilderness near the Mogollon Rim, looking up at the stars. They filled the sky like a bowl of tiny pebbles hanging upside down, unaffected by gravity. I was baptized in their tiny pinpricks of light, which washed gently over my skin. Then I realized that their light was wet and I was being washed in grief – the grief of missing their presence. I kept my eyes open, overflowing as they were with tears, and in my peripheral vision I saw a woman with flowing gray hair approach me. She moved with grace and sensuality, at home in her voluptuous body. When she reached me, she stood next to me and wordlessly looked up at the sky, a witness to the beauty. She held my grief in her own heart; that was more comfort than I thought possible.

I did not say anything. I did not explain or brush away my tears. But she *knew*.

Dream in a Starless City

During city-hushed hours trickled
with sirens, engines, an occasional
train, I dream of a night sky, kalamata-
black, trellised with constellations,
all the stars in between.

I cried as each needle of light grew
brighter, stitching familiar limbs,
scales, lynx, fish and all my
imagination could sketch
in a few solid moments of night.

The city sank in the periphery
and a woman rose beside me.
Her gaze, a benediction. She was
not surprised by the torrent of tears
and said only, I know. I know. I know.

She said it like the rhythm of a drum beating deep in my heart. She said it until I could feel the truth of being known in my body. She said it over and over and over. And she did know. She held my grief in such tender hands. She held me in the womb of the world.

After a long time and as the sun was beginning to rise, she took me down a trail into a dawn-lit meadow, shadowed with deep purples and indigos, paisley over the earth. The grasses were high, their seed-ed tips refracting the first of the sun. The oaks and maples that lined the meadow were golden. Their robes were changing as they prepared to shed them. Her voice, deep and melodious as a cello, rose with a song, the song with which she greets the day. She let go of my hand and moved across the open field toward a waiting fire. And then she beckoned me to join her. I sat beside her on a jewel-toned quilt. She smelled like earth and twilight and wildflowers and cinnamon and last night's stars. Silvered threads wove and wandered gracefully over the fabric. On the underside of the quilt were tiny sewn pockets, for tucking away secrets and prayers. I was warmed, through and through, by the fire. My tears dried like cornflowers on my face.

Hildegard of Bingen says that "with an embrace and a kiss the human being is released from the depth of God's heart and sent into the womb of the world." While I began this search imagining that mysticism was simply a commoner's attempt to perceive and engage with the Real, I have landed again and begrudgingly in the realm of theology. In my experience and imagination, the center and gravity of mysticism is belovedness. It is not so much about submitting to God, as mystical theology written and described largely by men assumes, but rather about a sense of belonging and collaboration with the divine.

I, for one, cannot fathom my belovedness some days – even though I have known it in my dreams. But I want to know it more – while I heat water in the morning for tea, wrap our children in blankets to steal away the chill, weep for starlight, wrestle through sleepiness, make breakfast and open my eyes to chaos and mess and city. I wonder if belovedness is where we must reside if we are to live the mystic's life – both through inviting others into that sense of being beloved and abiding there ourselves – and it is a harder path than I expected.

Unlike the grim spirit of perfectionism that can accompany old mystical practices, if the center of mysticism is belovedness, it requires not sacrifice or effort, but simple acceptance, *presencing*. It could mean clearing an internal meadow in the midst of the chaos and abiding there for a moment or two. It can be the hardest thing in the world to simply receive – to open yourself up to what is.

My son, Jude, turned to me in bed this morning as we relished the time just before dawn and said, "Mama, is it winter today?" He feels the shift in the earth and air, away from summer, and doesn't know the name for what comes next. I told him it was autumn, when the leaves begin to fall. I love the leaves so much for their falling because I know what it means to be loosed from the branches that you thought were required for survival. I know the terror and the dance of the fall. I know the feel of the cold earth beneath me. I know what it is to be decreated into that very soil, abandoned part by part, cell by cell, into the shadowed heart of the earth, into the heart of God. It is terrifying, but it is what I wake for.

Aaron took both boys to the park a couple of blocks away. I watch them waddle down the street taking tiny steps. I smile. It's going to take an hour to get there at that rate. But one of the beautiful things about Aaron is that he doesn't mind moving slowly through a day. I stayed home because I'm sick. I stayed home to watch the autumn light pour through our front window. The sun barrels in differently today. Its strokes are longer, dimmer. The dark is coming. The birdsongs are sparser. I can almost smell the snow to come, feel the shadows that will creep over the earth. We are tilting away from sun into shadow. Autumn creeps closer and my heart leans toward the movement of the wind and the tilt of the earth and in that place, I turn toward a moving image of God.

Turning toward a moving image of God as The Living Wind or turning toward an image that implies uncertainty such as The Depths is a significant move and one I want to explore and live into. It is admitting, with our very language, that the divine needs more space. It is part of the terror and dance of the fall. If I call God "Breath," I can feel God within me and without. But by calling the divine "Breath," I am recognizing that the divine is uncontainable. That is entirely the point, of course, and yet it can feel threatening to those of us accustomed to tight containers for God. But it also reminds us that a mystical path is an experimental path by its very nature.

Perhaps in every new season of life, as every cycle begins its long slow circling around us, we are invited to find the divine anew. I want to distinguish this pursuit from faith, which is reliant on belief. I am speaking, instead, to direct experience. It is my longing to know the divine, not merely to believe in the divine. [56] But unlike dogma, direct experience is inherently uncertain. Perhaps because my paradigm is less around belief, I experience the divine differently as I change. The face of the divine changes. I use different names as I need God differently. Often these changes are initially disorienting – it can feel like I have lost God. But I wonder if the divine is too alive to remain static. God changes, perhaps not in essence, but in shape and color and form, like the late autumn light harkens us toward winter, preparing us for what is to come.

If mysticism is in fact non-directional, which I believe it is, then mysticism inherently asks me to let the names and symbols and constructs I have around God fall away – time and again. As the 13th century mystic, Meister Eckhart said, "And so I ask of God that [God] make me quit of God." [57] Time and again, mysticism challenges fixed dogmas and doctrines and their inherent power structures. Mysticism challenges the importance our society has placed on belief. It does not trap the divine but rather opens up a meadow in which I can hope to meander and circle and explore. But it is a meadow that also sometimes gets dark.

Rilke says, "It is an experimental path by which we find ourselves lured into 'the open.'" [58] And in this open that is sometimes inky and unlit, in the solace of the bare and silent places, I want to reach for the divine through reaching for what God is not or put another way, what I do not know about God.

There is an entire framework and theological tradition that orbits around what God is not, called apophatic theology. Apophatic theology is also described as negative theology or *via negativa*. It is a manner of thinking and spiritual practice that approaches God, or the divine, by negation, speaking only in terms of what cannot be said about God. It empties us of inadequate images and "boldly deconstructs every human attempt to capture and contain a God who dwells in thick darkness." [59] It is also a helpful interpretive framework for women when traditional God symbols lose meaning for them. [60] This way is a profound relief to me when I cannot even begin to say what or who God may be. And only through this back door of what God is not, have I sometimes experienced God again. This makes me think about how one of my dear friends from childhood said to me recently and astutely that I would have to enter in through a back door if I ever wanted to be a part of a church again. If it's not yet obvious, I do love back doors.

My head and heart are full of questions. There is so much I cannot say about The Living Wind. As autumn moves through me, as I reckon with the rains, I feel like I am being forced into underground currents. I am grieved at how it seems like it is so much easier to cause harm than good. In my work in Armenia, I have three residents whom we brought to their supposed forever home, but they are not home. They are in the institutions, the places we were trying desperately to avoid when we started this work. And no matter what I do, it is not enough to bring them home. I cannot live without causing harm, even if accidental and unknowingly. I do not know how to make progress with this great impasse or the one Aaron and I are experiencing around where to live.

Chant of Rain

When rain falls in the city,
nothing grows except
underground currents.

Furious, it rushes toward
one seaward outlet, pushes
through me into clogs

of fallen leaves, tortured
plastics. I have missed grounds
soaked with sky and aging

aspen bark disrobed
to colors of harvest moons,
autumnal suns, once a year,

end of self, barrier between
body and world, matter
against matter

against me. Now I know
I cannot live without
causing harm. From here

can I walk back into the heart
of my own life, disappear
finally into my own furious

impasse? Is mysticism simply
how days pass through me,
absorb into skin, pass through

me, resurrected?

Mysticism right now is my attempt to walk back into the heart of my own life and belovedness on a daily basis. The way that I am trying to carve out and create is not one that assures direct experiences with the divine, but rather cultivates the soil so that this might be possible. But that is all we can do. I think of Annie Dillard's words in *Holy the Firm* when she says, "Every day is a god, each day is a god, and holiness holds forth in time. I worship each god, I praise each day splintered down, splintered down and wrapped in time like a husk, a husk of many colors spreading, at dawn fast over the mountains split." This is the meadow that I want to live within – where dawn fast over the mountains splits, where experience is more powerful than doctrine and matter rubs up against soul, where the inner light is more important than religious authority and where the voice within is more powerful than those that speak from the pulpit or the pages of books, even this one. And I can only hope that this will be a comfort as I surrender to places of descent, shadow and confusion as portals to the divine.

In the meantime, it is Halloween and Jude is going to be a pumpkin for the second year in a row. Silas will be a teddy bear. We're going to open our home to our neighbors and friends for a simple dinner of chili. We will build a fire out back and serve apple cider and mulled wine. It should be a special night, even on two hours of sleep, even sick, even city-bound.

Shadow

To go in the dark with a light is to know light.
To know the dark, go dark. Go without sight,
And find that the dark, too, blooms and sings,
And is traveled by dark feet and dark wings.

— Wendell Berry[61]

It is not just matter or dust or our bodies that are portals to the divine, but also places of confusion and shadow. If I want to dig for God in the ore of my own life, in the earth, animals, sky, then I also must mine for God in the silent places, the shadowed places, the places of unknowing – maybe, even especially, there. There are numerous times in my own life when the divine has not been felt or seen or heard or known. In her poem, "Mystic", Sylvia Plath writes:

The air is a mill of hooks –
Questions without answers,
Glittering and drunk as flies
Whose kiss stings unbearably
In the fetid wombs of black air under pines in
summer.

The world is not one of pines in summer, but it is full of questions without answers. As I fall into bed soon after the boys go to sleep my mind catches and whirlpools with the questions: *Where will we go from here? How will we escape this city intact? How will we live when death has painted in broad strokes over the sunlight?* I fall into a fitful sleep despite the way my body aches with weariness. Lately it feels like I have growing pains again like I had as a child – deep aches inside my legs, bones throbbing.

Just as I sink into a deeper sleep and a dream begins of highways and roundabouts, Silas wakes up to nurse. I calm myself with the knowledge that I have gone to bed early; there is plenty of time ahead to sleep. He nurses quietly, rubbing the fabric of my sweatshirt between his fingers. He falls asleep and I sink almost immediately into sleep and pick up where my dream left off, driving too quickly on a roundabout, fearing the car will spin out of control. At some point, I sense that Aaron has come to bed. He slips into bed quietly and just as my breathing deepens, Silas wakes again to nurse. I sigh and my eyes sting with tears. All. I. Want. Is. Sleep. But his new teeth are coming in. His mouth is sore and swollen and nursing is all that relieves his pain. I nurse him. I rub his back. He falls back to sleep. Aaron starts snoring. I nudge him awake and ask him to roll over. I try to settle into sleep. I push aside the questions; I try to go anywhere but back to that roundabout of my dream, but there it is, a freeway roundabout high in the sky this time, making it more dangerous if I were to spin out of control. I don't know which exit to take but finally choose one just to be done with the spinning. I'm not sure how much longer I can hold the steering wheel steady. Silas cries out in his sleep, reaches for my body.

As he nurses, I grit my teeth. I moan from the pain of fatigue. Aaron hears and tries to take Silas downstairs. He can tell I am close to my edge. Silas screams for twenty minutes. He wakes up Jude. I cuddle Jude back to sleep for a few minutes and the ease of his body falling back to sleep is a tender comfort. The tears and screams continue downstairs. Since I cannot sleep anyhow, I go downstairs and tell them to just come back to bed. And we nurse again; I fall asleep this time before he is even finished and there in my dream is the exit I have chosen but it has a toll to pay. I reach into my wallet. It is empty.

Silas wakes again. It feels like some form of torture to be awoken nearly every half hour. I fear I will lose my mind if it happens again. I will scream like an animal in pain. I have done it before. So, I crawl out of bed and strap this ten-month-old babe to my chest in the worn carrier and walk the house in the dark until he is asleep. Aaron finds us in the morning, sleeping on the couch, Silas still strapped to me. My eyes are swollen. My limbs are aching.

A little while later, I slowly walk the two blocks to the café and open my journal to this line by Robert Frost: "We dance round in a ring and suppose, but the secret sits in the middle and knows."[62] How will I discover the secret? How will I know what it knows? I think of the circular exit in my dream. The secret sits in the middle and knows while I circle it, out of control.

It is winter, again. We have circled around and the café window awakens into grey. I wanted to stay in the light of summer, the bounty of autumn. I wanted to write about a mysticism of the light. But the only slender scrap of sky that is visible to me is a weary grey, as are the concrete sidewalk slabs, the asphalt, the pillars and arches of the raised train line, the storefronts behind them. And I have no way to spread light into the shadows – not my own or others. The windows across the street are grey-black as is the car parked nearby and the jackets and sweaters of the locals walking by with the grey-shine of their smartphones that creates a blue-grey reflection on their faces. Where are the colors? The mud speckles the sides of a claustral-grey car, and the pants of the man who just entered. If I stay here much longer, all my poems and words will be the same moribund grey, the same geometric designs of apartment windows, bank logos, tailgates, bricks.

This is the grey of city, the grey of January, the grey of post-Industrialism, the grey of morning. This is the grey of melting snow. This is the ashen grey of sadness and fatigue. And I wonder about the grey of mysticism. Last week, my spiritual director, Vivienne, said to me, "There is a mysticism of lights up and lights down and both are equally bewildering." I think by this she meant that there are times when the lights are on, figuratively speaking, and we can blessedly see around us and not trip over some large boulder jutting up from the trail. When the lights are up, we understand. Perhaps joy is close at hand, if not enveloping us. Perhaps we feel the touch of the divine. We know what the next step should be and we can take it, we can put one foot in front of the other. The mysticism of lights down speaks to the times that we are fumbling around in impenetrable places, when shadows loom large and we cannot make sense out of any of the shapes and sights around us. We are afraid. Perhaps our days are characterized by absence. We don't know anything at all.

Today, I am learning the mysticism of neither lights up nor down, but the grey area in between. The texture of mysticism and the way we move through the world is different depending on whether all is grey, lit or dark. But one experience does not actually make more sense than the other. It can be just as perplexing to see as to not see. So, I agree with Vivienne. All three places are equally bewildering.

Every night we ask the questions at dinner: *What gave you life today? What took away life?* We ask these questions to notice the Mystery in our days, in the giving and the taking. We ask these questions so that we can recognize the sacred in the clacking of the tree branches in winter wind, in the exhaustion and dragging fatigue and headaches.

But maybe we are asking these questions for the wrong reason. Maybe it is less about whether God is there in the giving and the taking and more about whether or not we are showing up in our own lives. How are we to read the signs of our own lives? Rather than worry (as I do) about twisting or misreading these signs, we need to simply notice and value our lives' strange signs, the abiding FarNear, the roundabouts and circular paths. I first heard the term FarNear as one name for God in Anne Carson's *Decreation*. She says: "There is no clear boundary between far and near; there is no climactic moment of God's arrival."

The days are bluntly cold. New York City temperatures fell to a record low of 4°F this morning. It broke a 116-year record. Tiny dustings of snow and wind are an icy hand on my face. The bitter cold has meant that my children have not played outside in weeks. *The air is a mill of hooks.* It is not just weariness and exile and the inability to make a decision about our future home that drags at my limbs, but loss and death. For today I am content to stay underground with the flowers, marking time.

Death

Death and life are so woven together that they
are completely indistinguishable:
you cannot see one without the other.

— Christian Wiman [63]

Less than two years ago, when I found out I was pregnant with Silas, my sister had also just conceived. We were pregnant together with only the distance of the width of the nation between us. Our babes were due two weeks apart, come autumn. Deep down inside, I think we both knew we were carrying boys before it was possible to confirm such things.

Just as our tummies began to bulge like soft peaches, my sister started bleeding. That terrifying day was the beginning of more than two months of fear and bewilderment. And in that time the distance between us began to stretch out and lengthen. I tried to measure the distance in so many ways, in how far a person could walk in an hour, and in that case, we were 800 leagues apart and I would have had to walk through the middle country between us – through plains and fields of corn, sunlight shuffled through husks into sweet kernels would strip my body dry. But I was not supposed to walk that far given my own precarious pregnancy with Jude, given that I was already dilated and my body was tempted to push this babe out too early. So, I stayed in Queens for a while longer and listened to the cadence of grasshoppers at dusk. This was my lonely music while my sister laid flat in a hospital bed, hands cupped around her peach-round belly, her little girl at home with her husband, asleep in their beds.

The sweetness of the chromatic scales of the growth for these two babes was lost and instead, I started watching the way grief has many shades, the ways a smile can harden in an instant, fear a sheath. I couldn't see my sister's face but I could smell terror in her voice, could hear the downturn at the end of each sentence. She wasn't sleeping well. All those days in the hospital were days snatched from her and her tiny daughter.

I wanted to ward it all off. At night I would slowly walk the back garden over to the corner lot with the yard stashed with trash bags and every form of litter imaginable. I stayed there looking at apple peels that fought their way back to earth through inviolable plastic. I thought of my sister. I tallied my steps home, less than one league. I unsnagged my hair from mulberry branches, unsnagged hope. Is it true that each beauty harbors a hidden wasteland?

Finally, I crossed the plains between us and made my way to Arizona for the summer. Each mile I drove was a sacrament to what I knew would be shared grief if it came to that.

Weston Max was born on July 7, 2012 at 24 weeks. He was tiny and perfect and sweet. There was only a brief crest of three weeks between his birth and his death. I was there the day he first opened his eyes. I looked hard into those stormed clouds. I was choked by the weight of his labored breathing. But my sister's hands on his body, tending his flawless form, were stunning. She was unafraid to love. This is the picture of tenderness: her eyes, only for him in that maze of machinery clanging, PICC procedures, and new vocabulary to measure lungs and each drop of milk she leaked.[64] I did not know him nearly long enough – but the rise and fall of his chest, his silent cries, and finally sleep under the wings of my sister's hands, these things I will never forget.

I only touched him after he had died.

No Rhythm

Breath was two clouds fighting
                                across desert skies
ocotillo strangled the day you died.

The nurse came to check
your scant heartbeats—

she wanted to write down the time
                                (of your death)
That sentence
                is impossible to close.

Curled next to my sister's heart,
the first aria her body sang you
                                was the last one
                        you heard.

That day
Arizona was the bottom of an inland sea.

I want to write down your hands—

grasping my finger even after
                you slipped through,
        the way they achingly alighted
on my sister's palm like a Pieridae—
                small white butterfly,

the palmar grasp reflex—
        hands were meant to hold.
I held yours as much as decency would allow.

We just returned from Arizona again. We had not been back since Weston died and since Silas was born. We stayed with my sister and her family and reckoned with Weston's absence sharpened by Silas' presence. Each morning, Silas would toddle out to the kitchen and his uncle who should have been holding a little boy about the same size would sweep him up and hold him on his hip all morning long. I sat on the couch drinking my tea, trying not to watch, trying not to cry, not tasting the tea, the toast catching in the back of my throat.

At night, when my sister and I sat on the couch and I would inevitably need to nurse Silas all I could feel was the emptiness of her arms, the smallness of her breasts. My own body was numb.

Nothing about this will ever add up. We moved in and out of the pain while we were together, blinded. And that too is a mystical practice – not the kind that we want to have, perhaps, but the shadowy, slow and begrudging kind. And though I am home now, the same cold steals through my body. The lights are out. It is death. It is bewildering. The felt absence of consolation in this place of grief sends me into the wild.

The combination of the death of my nephew and the birth of my son still push me to the edge of myself and into another realm entirely where my mind feels foggy and close to splitting open at others. But it is a cruel truth – that the feeling in the room where Weston died was not that different than the feeling in the room when Silas was born. Death and birth are terribly and gorgeously intertwined. They are intimates; they are the borderlands. And the feeling in both rooms, in both places, was that of longing – sacred and ordinary both.

Death stole from my son through his womb-time and his first year. The stones of grief in my stomach dismantled the light that should have belonged to him. It was a season of dust and nothing flowered. Even as his movements pushed up against my ribs, they were not as real as my nephew's cold skin on mine, his diminutive bones that withstood the weight of one of my kisses, the heartbeats that were buried. Sometimes I don't even know if I can bear the joy of Silas' sooty eyes.

I, in fact, gasped when his breath finally stayed. And this too, is a loss that unravels the seams of my heart. Often, when I have felt momentarily lost in the joy of loving Silas, I am abruptly overcome with guilt because my fullness is my sister's emptiness. He has had to steal my heart. And it took a while. I wasn't able to give it to him.

As Elizabeth Robinson says, it is the charge of a parent "to live on the unraveled edges of death and stitch them together as regeneration." [65] I wish I knew how to do just that. Weston is with God in something like spirit and rising and air. Silas is with God in matter – through bodies and hands and breath. There is nothing about this that makes any sense. I am not trying to explain it. I am not trying to make it beautiful. I am trying to live with it and not lose God entirely.

In Dreams I Am Someone Else, Mostly You

You are still a family of four
in those hours before dawn tinctures,
when impurities burn off and even I

forage through sleeplessness.
You came to our childhood home last
weekend, grief clotted in your throat.

At the bottom of the stairs, I stood,
silent, in the shaft of morning
where I first knew he had died.

I looked at you and remembered
my arms wrapped our mother's
thin waist as she leaned over, braced,

her hand cradled the phone.
All she had to say was, "Oh, Jesus"
and I knew. We were split down

the middle. I am still not sure
what happened to you in that instant.
It has been less than two weeks

and maybe even you cannot know
the bottom of this mountain of loss.
I almost said kaleidoscope of loss,

but this is not beautiful. And
this is not pebbles, or beads, or
bits of glass mirrored and patterned.
This is death.

Silas' life will always be connected to Weston's death. If I deny the Mystery in the fate of one of them, do I deny the Mystery in the other? I want to believe that the Mystery is with them both and all around, but I wrangle with doubt. I rage. It is desperately unfair.

My sister and I are worlds apart right now. I sent her Clarissa Pinkola Estés' book, *A Faithful Gardener*, which I thought would be a comfort in this time. She never mentioned it to me, but I saw on her blog that she loved it. She has been bonding over it with someone else who lost a child. I do not know why this hurts as much as it does. But it does.

She can hardly look at me when I am holding Silas. And believe me, sometimes I can hardly bear to be myself. Nowadays she no longer calls or writes me back regularly. But when we do talk on the phone, I try to be gentle. I try to ask questions about her heart, her loss, her son. And she answers, but so briefly. Grief is a wild maze and I know she is lost in it. I cannot blame her. She does not ask me often about Silas and I usually do not offer anything, and then sometimes at the very end of the conversation, she will pause and then ask, "How is Silas?" And I answer in three words or less, "He is well." And I feel like I just mean something like "He is alive" and she, of course, knows it. Then there is an awkward silence that we do not know how to fill. I filter out the milestones that will just make her heart break all over again. I filter out so much that I end up grieving the fact that she does not know my son. She didn't call on his first birthday, which I understand, and which aches just the same. Her heart had to have splintered again with her own loss on the day Silas was born. I don't know how she bore that news, but I can only imagine that it seared and burned. And I imagine that it feels hard to celebrate what you wish you had. I do not know how long grief will lock us into this distance. But I know that I will wait. I know that it is worth it.

I read her blog which catalogs and chronicles her pregnancy with Weston, his life and death and what has come after. This is the first time she has ever had a blog. She mentions in a post that she misses me right now and that we are distant. Maybe I just don't understand blogs, but I want to scream and tear out my hair. I want to understand why she can write this on a blog and not say it to me. And even as I say that, I know I cannot understand. I hope I never understand. So instead, I weep bitter tears that I cannot mend the distance. She is reaching out to people who have lost a child not those of us who have gained one. I feel her slipping away and do not blame her. She is searching for God in stories of death. I must, because my son breathes, also search for God on the side of life. Clearly, in this, I am the lucky one.

I wonder sometimes if I feel something akin to survivor's guilt. I do not know how to integrate these side-by-side experiences of life and death. I do not know what mysticism means here, except the mysticism of lights down. And what can I do within the mysticism of lights down except sit in the shadows and wait?

But in this unlit place, in the longing around the hours of life and death, I am hoping that these longings are God's. Ever so occasionally, I feel subject and object fall away in this place. Is it the sacred heart that grieved to hear Weston's eulogy? Is it the sacred heart that was not ready to buttress the sap-dark hours against Weston's leaving? Is it the sacred heart that knows these mangled days where we are all left breathing, but just barely? I hope so. Somehow that is the tiniest of consolations when every blossom, every cry reminds me of Weston's tiny round mouth bleating silently.

Birth

Life rises out of death, death rises out of life; in being
opposite they yearn to each other, they give birth
to each other forever and are forever reborn.

— Ursula LeGuin [66]

Before Silas was born, I wrote a short poem, a prayer, if you will. I wanted to find a way to bless his birth before we entered into that space, since it felt so crowded with death and loss.

Wishes for Childbirth

To dive into a quiet pond
and resurface with you—

bloom of goldenrod,
my late autumn harvest.

To speak not of death—
the unbearable stillness.

To hear nothing but song
in your first cry.

To hold you up to innocent
skies, spun, scattered

like a globed dandelion
flecked with sunrise and dew.

To hear lungs that bloomed
like secrets underwater.

To stand beneath these trees
catching sparks with bare hands—

galaxies of leaves.

It didn't turn out quite like that, the galaxy of his birth. But some parts of that prayer were answered, to be sure.

The common usage of the word prayer is far too limited. I did not pray in the midst of Weston's struggle and life and death, as we normally understand it, or through Silas' birth. I couldn't. Both were places without words. But when I look back at those hours, they were, in fact, prayers – the prayers of the hours. The liturgies were the movements of my body as I leaned over Weston's and then again as I brought my son into the world. Sometimes mysticism is action – especially when every fiber of our physical beings is engaged in the prayers of life and death.

I cannot speak to the prayers of my sister's body in this time but I imagine that they had something to do with the song she sang Weston as he died and in her shielding hands over his body. I imagine that they had something to do with the miles and miles she ran and hard after he died. But I do not know for sure. However, I can elaborate on the prayers of my own body during the labor and delivery of my second child. Given the grief and survivor's guilt and death and loss which swirled around my pregnancy, when it finally came time to birth him, I was afraid to surrender. I was afraid to allow my body to open, though I knew it was *time*, though my body moved headlong and fast in that direction, though I wanted him desperately. In the maze and beauty of somatic intelligence, my own inner conflicts became outer conflicts and translated into weak contractions. I knew I needed to let the contractions overtake me. I knew surrender was in order.

Aaron and I were crouched on the floor of our living room, a thrifted chunky light-grey wool rug beneath us to soften the hardwood floors, to warm us. It was late autumn and the middle of the night and I could only bear to have candles lit in our home. Any other light was too glaring and invasive. The midwife and doula came quickly; they could tell by my voice that this was moving fast. They came into our home wordlessly and joined Aaron and I on the floor sensing quiet was needed. They crouched silently and just watched in the dark, unmoving and loving witnesses.

With these three brave souls beside me now, I tried to move through labor. But there was so much holding me back – memories of the NICU, the way I could barely breathe at Weston's funeral, the way I tried to hide my pregnant stomach under a loose black dress that pinched my arm pits, and my sister's heartbreak. I couldn't do anything about these things. I knew that. And yet, I couldn't get past them.

I also couldn't get past my own fear. What if my babe dies during childbirth? What if he dies just like Weston did? Death was more real, more tangible, more etched into the memories of my body, than anything else. Hospital corridors, elevators, and the all-pervasive death were the landscape of every dream I had about my own babe. I needed courage – courage I didn't think I had, courage to bring forth life. And they could tell.

Kristin, our midwife, said simply, "Natalie, you must let these contractions take over. You have to let them be big. You must choose life." I had no strategies in place for this next act. No one had talked about this in the birthing class or written about this in a book, so I found myself opening my hands, literally, in the brief moments of rest between contractions. All I had available to me was this physical act of surrender, that I hoped would coax my body into surrender. All I had was the knowledge that I must keep my hands open as much as possible. And I had tears – so many tears.

As the contractions finally took over, Mary Esther, our doula put her hand on my hair as I wept. I didn't weep for physical pain as there was almost no physical pain in this birth. I think it might have been overshadowed by the more real and more acute grief and rage I felt for all that had been taken, for *who* had been taken. Mary Esther whispered something akin to a lullaby, much like you would over a child who is crying. Kristen discreetly slipped towels beneath me. Aaron's hand stayed on my shoulder. No one spoke. This was my prayer for my son and all his life or death would mean. This was a prayer for myself and all that must shift and open and break within me in the act of loving and mothering. This was a prayer for Weston, a crying out on his behalf. This was a prayer for my sister – for all that death had taken from her. This was even my prayer for the world – tinged as it was with death on this late autumn night.

And in the midst of it all, in between the grief and rage and worry, my body prayed and pleaded, *let him be alive*. Let him be. Let him come forth.

There are many forms a divine child can take. There are efforts and births that are not literal that require their own varied forms of prayers. But this one was human, wrapped in flesh, coursing, blessedly, with breath and blood.

Encounter

Let us pray dangerously.
Let us throw ourselves from the top of the tower,
let us risk a descent to the darkest region of the abyss,
let us put our head in the lion's mouth and,
direct our feet to the entrance of the dragon's cave.

— Regina Sara Ryan [67]

Karl Rahner said that the only way a person will survive with an intact faith in this century is by being a mystic. I interpret what he said to mean something about how many of us are no longer able to have faith and hold onto faith through the channels of authority, or even, perhaps through belief. There has to be a direct experience – a lived encounter with the Mystery. There needs to be contact with the Spirit of the Universe. And if that contact is not had, then God will be lost to us.

That rings true of my experience. These years have been steeped in descent – in the moldy leaves decaying, in the many years of living in what has felt like exile, in real heart-stopping death, in new life, in starless skies. And religious authority has not provided a way through. I go to an Episcopal church, very occasionally, and sometimes even experience it as an ascent, as *lights up*. There are candles and incense. There is organ music and voices are joined together. There are assertions and questions. There is a path through the year that is marked by different religious holidays. But I remain in the shadows. I remain on the outside, hemmed out by my own sensibilities.

But still, I am steeped in prayers – just not the kind that require kneeling, unless you count kneeling to scrub the kitchen floor. The last time I went to the Episcopal church, I heard the creeds as prayers, statements of belief. But they did not touch my heart. I do not want to assert belief as much as experience the sacred. I do not want to lay claim to theologies as much as be laid hold of. The prayers I know these days consist of curses under my breath when another glass of milk spills on the floor, the ways I try to listen every time my son says "Mama" and in listening to the stillness that comes with snow falling. And there are some prayers I don't even recognize as such. In Adélia Prado's poem "Mural", she talks about a woman collecting eggs and says:

> It's she who gives birth
> to nature's veiled radiance,
> it's her own delight
> in having a family,
> loving her agreeable routine.
> She doesn't know she knows
> the perfect routine is God:
> the hens lay their eggs,
> she lays out her skirt,
> the tree in due season
> displays those rosy blossoms.
> The woman doesn't know she's praying:
> Lord, let nothing change. [68]

If prayer is bringing my full self to the divine, then the work of my hands, the habits of my days, the giving and receiving, the blessing and cursing, anger and joy, silence and speaking are also a part of that prayer, whether I know it or not. It is part of an infuriating prayer that Aaron and I are at an impasse when it comes to leaving or staying in New York City. It is prayer each time we go and look at a house that is for sale wondering if this is the place our family should put down roots. It is prayer when I hang up the phone and weep after a phone call with my sister. Margaret L. Mitchell puts it like this:

Sometimes,

When it is all, finally,

too much,

I climb into my car,

roll the windows up,

and somewhere between

backing out of the driveway

and rounding the first corner,

I let out a yell

that would topple Manhattan.

How do you pray?

Oftentimes, I still can't help but think of prayer as something that takes effort and that wells from within us. Old habits die hard, I suppose. My default is to assume that when I'm stuck, for instance, and unable to make a decision or see a way out, that I should stop what I'm doing, clear internal space, reach toward the divine, reach, even for peace. My default is to over-function, to assume that if my labor contractions are not large enough to birth my baby that I should try harder.

But experience is showing me that prayer may begin in surrender to Mystery's longing for us (our belovedness, in other words) and end in the object of longing, which is ourselves. In prayer, we are not the acting agent, the responsible one. So, in this very hour, as I sit here wondering how we will find a way forward, I am trying to practice resisting the impulse to take responsibility even for finding an answer. Instead, I wonder about the longing of the sacred for me and toward me, the Mystery's longing for a life that makes sense for me. In this space, instead of the assumption that I need to find a way forward, I can rest, even if just for a moment, in this peace of being beloved, in this idea that I am the object of God's longing, as are Aaron and my boys. And for this moment, just for this one brief minute, that is enough.

Today it is just an idea, a deep hope. I do not know it viscerally or concretely and it feels more distant than I would like, but even the hope brings me some measure of peace that I was missing. And I hold those times close when I have known it viscerally, like when the Mystery showed up in my dreams offering me consolation and understanding when I was missing the stars.

Maybe this is prayer – not asking, but receiving. Not efforting but just staying present to my own belovedness. Teresa of Avila says, "The less we do, the more our efforts are quieted, the more of God we can sense, the more God can move toward us."

Midnight

God is invisible, distant, dwelling in darkness.

— 1 Kings 8:12

I said to my soul, be still, and let the dark come upon you
which shall be the darkness of God.

— T.S. Eliot [69]

I would have liked to write about light, as opposed to grey. I would have liked to write about shining, transcendent experiences of the divine. But there are plenty of people who have chronicled mysticism as light and fewer still who have allowed mysticism to remain in the sphere of the mundane and grey world that I live in, not to mention the mysticism of the shadows. So, I claim the path of a lost mystic as my own and willingly stay in the underground. I wade into the deep waters of suffering, death and unknowing and try to remain present to these unlit places, in the continued hope that there is a mystical path that does not require clarity, in the hopes that the shadows, absence, exhaustion, uncertainty and unknowing that are a part of me are also a part of the Mystery. That's a long list, I realize. That's a lot to hope for.

Our names of God, our ways of speaking of the sacred, attempt to make the invisible visible, or the unknowable known ever so slightly. But there are also seasons where there is no visible or tangible experience of the divine. There are seasons when mysticism is "a higher light still, not the light by which man 'gives names' and forms concepts…but the dark light in which no names are given, in which God confronts man not through the medium of things, but in [God's] own simplicity." [70]

I am not sure what it means to be a mystic in the shadows except that it doesn't feel good. It doesn't feel like I can lay claim to anything at all. But loss and death and life and confusion have landed me here in the shadows where no names are given. I am learning as I go what this may mean, and not for the first time.

There have been other seasons of utter desolation in my life – around depression and exile, abuse and bearing witness to unspeakable human suffering, especially in the psychiatric institutions and in my work as an activist in Armenia. And then there is today, which is not desolation but where everything is covered in shadows. The light is dim and dull coming through my window. The prosaic scene is this. The window is old and scratched and crooked in its frame. Yesterday we had a sweet day, swinging at the park, reveling in their laughter at the simplest pleasures, but today my sons are whining non-stop. Silas' whines are wordless, high-pitched moans. Jude's are about not wanting a hummus sandwich for lunch. He had a typical Saturday morning crash. I'm beginning to notice that whenever we have French toast for breakfast (which we only do on Saturdays), the rest of the day is nightmarish for Jude (and the rest of us; let's be honest). He is easily agitated and uncomfortable. He only wants to consume sugar for the rest of his life (I mean, the day). He whines about everything. Aaron is moping around the house – angry that everything is turned inside out and messy (our feet turn black when we walk on our own floors), angry that there aren't enough job openings in philosophy, angry (though he won't say it) that I can't seem to will myself to want a life here long-term. My sister and her family are lost in the labyrinth of grief an entire nation away (it might as well be worlds) and I cannot reach them. And I am lost, too.

There are cracks in my heart, cracks in the worn white wall I have been staring at the last fifteen minutes. There are cracks in my family. I was away for a few days for a work trip and the homecoming has been hard. It always is. The kids are clingy (and whining, lest you forgot already). The nights – just awful. Last night I was up seven times. The idea is that the sacred can come in through the cracks, the vulnerabilities. There are a lot of cracks here. That's all I'm saying. Fatigue and exhaustion do not allow me to carry on as usual. Yet still I resist that this unraveling is my portal to the divine. No amount of efforting can put me back together again. No spiritual practice can give me back the hours of lost sleep or the hours I was away from these two sweet and needy creatures. These very hours are my ugly psalms and my powerful laments.

What does it mean to be a lost mystic or a mystic of the dark? What does it mean to be one who does not know the way forward in regard to putting down roots someplace, somehow? What does it mean to be a mystic who does not even know her own heart or what that means for her beloved? What does it mean to be a mystic who won't claim *belief* as a foundation?

Perhaps it is not that God is absent, though I think a good argument could be made for that. But I, for one, cannot see or feel or know God. Not today. Not many days, hard though I may try. I know I am not alone in this. And at the same time, I know that there are those who experience a deep consolation in times of desolation. There are those who even feel a stronger presence of the divine in great suffering. There is a long spectrum when it comes to direct experience and only the reader can locate and place herself or himself along it.

Wherever one falls, there is a unique mystical path available. There are as many kinds of mystics as there are people. Some people hear from God. I have never been that person. I have just, sometimes, *felt* God – felt a divine presence. But what about these times when I feel nothing at all? How do we understand these times of intense and utter silence, if you will? What do we do on days when we are completely undone by death – the real, awful breath-taking deaths and the shadows underneath the living, the caves within the mountain?

Maybe all we can do on days like this is cry (or stare at the wall) and let that be our prayer. It is impossible for me to know if, in times of death and loss, I have been as alone as I have sometimes felt. But however we may come to understand it, it can be very lonely. While not everyone experiences the absence or invisibility of the divine presence in times of despair, that has typically been the case for me. I have suffered not only due to the external factors of loss, but also due to the fact that it is so terribly quiet. I have to wonder: why the strange loneliness when we are already faced with the deafening silence of death, divorce, betrayal, addiction or abandonment? Why the exodus of God?

Exodus

No one can see My face, but I will protect you
with My hand until I have passed by you, and then
I will remove My hand and you will see My back. [71]

I never forget the backs of those I love.
Without Your face, rib-caged muscles,
the high-lighted tilt of scapulars must
be memorized more closely lest I forget

again in slurry of copper-mine runoff,
scabs and sluices on Battle Mountain;
in the grit of early morning markets
where the stench of fish chokes.

Last night's laundry threads bare and
I cast for Your face in each bunch
of watercress I strip with elementary hands.
Skin navigates two universes. I'm tired

of being protected and lately confess
in diagrams of pine straw, to even have
forgotten. In quiet I've forgotten.
The sun sets late. I beg: at least use only

night to cover my eyes. *Forgive me: I forget*
in gin, in all these parts of my body, within
and without. Where are You while I labyrinth
further from the center, skirt ripped,

cracked leather shoes full of melted sleet,
lashed strands of hair across my face
like rage. I've learned to shout out loud.
I wake up hungry every night.

Am I circling around to relying on You
who has used me hard, whom I want—
still—apart from watered-down wine?
Am I bold to want more?

This is not meant to be a conversation about theodicy or *where* (if anywhere) God is when we are stuck in the proverbial midnight. It is only meant to be a conversation about how (if at all) we can be mystics in the silence and the shadows – mystics of the dark. Are there compasses that we can feel for in the night, or do we task ourselves to drop any compass and stop trying to find our way home?[72]

Cedrus Monte speaks to the fact that some of us may continue to circle back around to what she names "shrines of darkness" for our entire lives. She says:

Experiences of despair and loss of connection – even after break-through, life-changing events, extensive analysis and a profound sense of communion with the forces of nature and spirit – have led me to believe, and growingly accept that my own path leads me repeatedly on pilgrimages to the inner shrine of darkness, not because I am morally deficient, not because I am depressed, and not because there's some form of enlightenment or personal maturation that I am just not 'getting.' Rather, I am led to the shrine of darkness because, in spite of a desire to consistently experience the peace and happiness of a certain spiritual liberation, the mournful face of God abides within me and wants to be seen, and loved, through my eyes. At this shrine I have learned to love when I experience nothing to love.[73]

Perhaps mysticism is just as much living in the shadows and abiding within the sacred darkness as it is anything else. After all, there are shadows all around and we have to find a way to live with them. After all, there is a mournful face of God that wants to be known and seen. Meister Eckhart calls God's darkness a "superessential darkness, a mystery behind mystery, a mystery within mystery that no light has penetrated."[74] The patriarchal and religious hierarchies of our time do not want darkness or shadows (and sometimes even mourning) anywhere near God. But mysticism always clashes with the hierarchies of the time and perhaps with this one as well.

I want to reiterate that darkness can be holy. There are multiple possibilities around how to interpret the silence or absence of God (including the unfortunate one of blaming the victim) but the only thing that makes sense to me right now is that the divine is within the shadows and the darkness even if it cannot be felt or heard. *Maybe darkness is sometimes the point.* Maybe silence is the point. Perhaps it is so silent because the divine is silenced by our suffering – steeped as God is in the earth and bodies and losses and death. Maybe absence is the point and I could let go of all the ways I want to experience the divine so that the divine can be known. Anne Carson said,

> *The best one can hope for as a human is to have a relationship with that emptiness where God would be if God were available, but God isn't... [God] is not available because [God is] not a being of a kind that would fit into our availability. [God is] 'not knowable' as the mystics would say.* [75]

The dark is often a time of undoing and unsaying. It is often apophatic in nature, when knowledge of the divine can only be had through negation. The apophatic is an essential counterpart to the cataphatic – obtaining knowledge of the divine through affirmation. In the realm of the cataphatic, articulation is available to us. But there are times when articulation is impossible and all that is available to us is the apophatic way. There are times when there is nothing left to affirm. [76]

Can I be present in this darkness without needing to change it? Can I be rudderless and lost and holy all at the same time? Muddy mysticism is not just about trying to see – to open one's eyes to the divine. It is not just about being seen. It is not just about finding one's way. It is also about not seeing, not having to see, being lost and aimless, and experiencing what is hidden.

Today I keep thinking about the day just after my nephew died. I was staying at my grandparents' home with Aaron and my son, Jude.

Gold Bath Taps for the Disappearing Stars

I draw a bubble bath for my son.
Gold taps, porcelain tub smooth as an isolette.

It is one day since my nephew died;
my sister is five miles away under smoke trees.

I pour milkweed bubbles like life
that has not been drained but given.

This is not what happens. Nothing
has been given and mercy is a black hole

that swallows stars at astonishing rates
creating cavities without light.

Meanwhile, my son, charmed by bubbles,
says in a voice muted by black matter:

Mama, this is such a beautiful day.

For my son, the light broke through in his first experience of a bubble bath. But for me it did not, and the contrast broke my heart open – that both could be true on the same day. I want my heart to remain this unbearably open. Joanna Macy said in an interview, "What is the heart for, if not for breaking?"[77] Nothing feels truer today than that statement.

Even when it is midnight, even when nothing has been given and mercy is a black hole, I remain a sanctuary of the divine – my skin and bones the frame and shingles of one of God's dark temples. My feminine body is a mystical text. All the loss and life and death I have carried in my body write a unique mystical text. Rowan Williams, is the former Archbishop of Canterbury – the leader of the Anglican Church in the United Kingdom. He is also theologian, and poet, and says that we give shelter to God, thus implying that the divine is vulnerable in us and in the world. In Anne Carson's poem *Aria of the Flames,* she takes this even further:

> *I am no more in danger of God.*
> > *God has entire need of me –*
> *where else*
> > *can God put*
> > > *God's nakedness,*
> *where else*
> > *can God put*
> > *God's emptiness,*
> > *where else*
> > *can God put*
> > *God's nothingness,*
> > *where else*
> > > *can God put*
> > > *God's endless end,*
> > > > *but*
> > > *in*
> > *me?*

Growing up in Christianity, with the concept of crucifixion as a central image, I sometimes wonder if God is crucified by the world again and again. That makes sense to me today, though little else does: God was vulnerable in Weston's small body and in my sister's when her breasts were still full and her arms empty. Perhaps that is the only thing that makes sense when I think of what it means to be a mystic of the dark. Perhaps allowing myself to feel forsaken by the divine and afraid in my own disappointment, rage, depression, ennui or loss is what it means to be a mystic of the dark. To continue entering into the fear and sense of forsakenness. In the Christian tradition, even God forsook God. So perhaps all that is possible is to draw near to the absence of God and stay with it. And not let go. Because even though it is not a consolation, it is divine. Because in her work on decreation, Simone Weil says that "God can only be present in creation under the form of absence." [78] I do believe that dark can have the same purifying qualities as light. I do believe darkness is as important as the light. I do believe that sometimes we come out the other side (of light or dark) distilled. Not always. But often enough to hope.

It is still winter. The silence and the long nights are weightier in this time. And as Rilke says, "It is possible: [the dark's] great strength / is breaking into my body. // I have faith in the night." [79] The work of the mystic is to bear, which also means to carry and to suffer.

On that last trip to Arizona after Silas was born and not even a year after Weston had died, it was early morning and my niece snuck into our room. We could hear Silas jabbering away in her father's arms, like he did every morning during that heartbreaking trip. She said to Aaron, "I hear Silas. Sometimes I hear my brother." She cupped her hand to her ear and said, "I don't hear him right now. I only hear God. Weston is probably sleeping."

Hunger

To love and bear, to hope till hope creates
from its own wreck the thing it contemplates.

— Percy Bysshe Shelley[80]

There is nothing like the wilderness of a soul, whether we live in the city or on a homestead deep in the forest. And today, I need courage to face that wilderness, to ask questions.

A City Poem that Contains
Every Kind of Wilderness

With skylight, overlapped circles
spread small wings.

My sister's next babe unsafely
tucked in the forest of her body

while my son nurses toward
surrender, hands palmed up.

How will we ever leave this city
intact? Sea-depth falls from skies.

Is it the Job whale
or marrow of fatigue

that spins each drop
into a quiet collection of pain?

Once I lived through
four years of matins

before being granted dawn.
Nearly spun dry in Nocturne cycles.

Flecks of those years arch
toward the flight of trains.

I am looking for one bird
to brave the rain.

A few nights ago, Aaron and I had another difficult conversation around the entrapment I feel living in such a huge city. We are both so sick of these conversations. In between the words and silences and deep sighs, in the words that were said and were taken back, it was clear that we both feel threatened in different ways. In the end, Aaron said that he has employed tunnel vision and has been willfully blind to what I have sacrificed so that he could continue on his career path unimpeded. It was a relief to hear his honesty. It took my breath away to have his eyes open to what this has meant to me. It scared me, too, the surge of intensity and pain I felt at this acknowledgment.

And now in the light of day, I consider the lengthy denial of this particular desire to leave the city. I consider the real and true generosity I have bestowed to Aaron in living in cities. I consider how both the sacrifices and the generosity are part of my identity. As a dear friend said, I have to travel both of these traits back to their origin to rightly understand what is unfolding now. Where did I begin to devalue desire? And how do I reclaim it as holy?

I am intrigued by the etymology of the word desire. *De sidere* means "from the stars." Desire means, in some sense, to await what the stars will bring. From this perspective, desire does not appear to originate from deep within our own souls or bodies as I have imagined. But rather, desire may be something outside of us that beckons and cajoles us to actually do the necessary (desired) thing, whatever that is. It is our work to usher that desire into the intimacy of the daily sphere of our lives.

Vivienne, my spiritual director, said the other day that it is possible that my desires are necessary in our life together, as a family. I hate to say it, but that astonished me at first. At least when it comes to the big desires. On a daily basis and when it comes to the smaller things, I am fairly comfortable saying what I want. But when it comes to the big things – the things that could change the course of our lives – it is very difficult for me. But when I imagine these desires of mine as possibly from the stars, they feel as important as Vivienne imagines them to be.

Although archetypes of masculine and feminine are inherently limiting, they are also occasionally informative. Archetypally speaking, the masculine and feminine are oriented differently. The masculine "I" is considered more autonomous or separate. The feminine "I" is defined in relation to others and is woven into a myriad of attachments and connections. I can see the beauty in both.

While I want to participate in this process of loosening the ties of gender from biological sex, one poignant biological illustration of this difference is micro chimerism. During pregnancy, the mother and babe exchange DNA and cells. The babe's DNA (and by proxy, the babe's father's DNA) can remain in a mother's body, brain and blood for decades. Even more astounding is the fact that the babe's DNA can actually fight illness inside a woman's body years after the babe's womb time.

While the web of attachments and connections that are woven around my life are meaningful and even beautiful, I have to work hard not to disappear into that web – giving too much, over-extending myself, and finding too much of my identity in doing so. In Kathleen Fischer's book, *Women at the Well: Feminist Perspectives on Spiritual Direction,* she says that a woman's error (perhaps sometimes blindness) is feeling worthless when she is not, self-loathing, not being able to protect her dignity, and not trusting herself. Of course, it isn't that simple. This can also be a man's trap and a woman's may in fact look quite different. But in my female body and soulscape, this rings true. And it is turning inward, moving slowly but surely toward the center to my belonging within the divine and in my own body that begins to heal my outward self, and ultimately our outer world.

This understanding feels like it is crashing into my life and into the carefully constructed existence Aaron and I have created. And I am afraid. I need to be the one bird willing to brave the rain. In the words of the poet, Marge Piercy, I need to "learn again to speak / starting with I / starting with We / starting as the infant does with [my] own true hunger / and pleasure / and rage."[81]

Speaking of working hard not to disappear into the web of

connections, Silas was up most of the night again nursing. He is
fussy and feverish whether in my arms or in Aaron's. For now, he is
in Aaron's. But I do not know how to move inward when there is so
much raw need reverberating through the house. I struggle with this
on a daily basis. Aaron does not. He can work here, in this closet of
a room, no matter what is going on downstairs. I am envious of that
ability to disconnect.

I know there is a daily and abiding tension between action and con-
templation, between reaching out and going within. We need both to
maintain soulfulness. Some of us need more of one than others. But
the world (and my children) will always ask for more than I am able
to give, even though I have tried so hard to whittle the world down
to something manageable. The world will still threaten to take over
every quiet moment.

The chorus of cries continues downstairs. The boys need me. And
they don't. For me, it is almost always easier to justify entering in
than remaining at a quiet distance. It is usually easier to sacrifice than
to not. But that is not what is always called for. For a little while this
morning, I am willing to step back from that sacrifice.

I have spoken in these pages of the grim spirit that can haunt a
man or woman's psyche around giving too much away. But some-
times that can also look like perfectionism. This grim spirit requires
watchfulness and careful tending so that I don't again go down that
path of disappearance. I must be willing to allow others to sacrifice.
Sometimes that means allowing them to hold the crying babe. And
maybe it means leaving New York City. I shudder at the thought and
am simultaneously jarred with hope.

Both are difficult (to sacrifice and to receive) and both taken to the
extreme will lead to a loss of self. But taken together, they are beau-
tiful. The sacred is here as I descend into the muddiness of my own
life and try to find a harbor here. The sacred is here when I step out
of the muddiness enough to see its glory and meaning.

And now, I will go downstairs and hold the still-crying babe because
I want to, because offering him comfort will soothe my body as well.

Emergency

*In the effort to reach a sacred place, the traveler must be guided by
a deep need (whether conscious or unconscious) to reach it.*

— Belden Lane [82]

Silas was nursing the other day, as babies do. We laid on the bed
on our sides. He finished nursing and sat up. We played together
for a few minutes. He leaned in to touch my face and then would
giggle and pull away. As he giggled and pulled away the last time,
he toppled over backwards and fell onto the hardwood floor, on his
head. Our pediatrician asked that we go to an emergency room in
Manhattan. It was my second time going to an emergency room with
Silas. The first was when he had the first of his seizures, which remain
unexplained to this day. And now this toppling over. Aaron stayed
home with Jude as we anticipated a long night.

We got to the hospital before nightfall. I stayed up with him all
night long as the dark settled over Manhattan, as the torchlights of
the city were raised and began to flicker. I kept watch as we waited
and waited. Due to his symptoms, the doctors were concerned about
a brain bleed. The stakes were high. I couldn't help but think of all
the death dreams I had while I was pregnant with him. I couldn't
help but wonder if we had cheated death, but only for a brief time. I
waited alone – life and death so closely intertwined – threads wind-
ing and unwinding on the same spool. It was too soon. I was still so
raw from the unexplained seizures, and more so from the past two
years of grief and loss and death – the death of my nephew, and the
death of my oldest friend's beloved seven-year-old son.

I held Silas down while the nurses tried and failed time and again
to insert the IV into his hands, his feet, his arms. Silas was already

in so much pain from the head injury that it was hard to allow the nurses to impart more pain onto his tiny body. He writhed in my arms. While the nurse took a break from trying to establish his IV, he laid on my chest, worn out and animal-like – trying to get as close to me as he could manage. It was as if he was trying to get back inside of me. But even I could not protect him from the pain.

Then they tried again. Thankfully, a gentle friend and neighbor was working at the hospital that night on a different floor. Knowing we were there, she took a break and came into our room. She placed her hands on Silas and on me through his screaming and my silent tears. I closed my eyes to his pain and held him and sang him songs until they were done, blessedly done. I will always be grateful for her hands upon us. I can feel them now.

We had many hours to wait for a CT scan, many hours in which I was not permitted to nurse him because his stomach had to be empty for the injection that would cause him to be still enough to complete the scan. This meant I could not comfort him as I usually would and in the way he naturally expected. He hardly slept while we waited. Instead he wept and wept and wept. It caused me physical pain every time he cried. He cried most of the night.

At one point, he was weeping and I was not permitted to hold him. So, I pressed my lips to his tiny cheek and placed my palm over the whole glorious cavity of his chest. I brooded. It was a divine posture of concern. Was the divine close to Silas in and through my body? I don't know, but I hope so. Teresa of Avila says that "Christ has no body now but yours. No hands, no feet on earth but yours. Yours are the hands with which he blesses all the world." [83]

The doctor came in to the room where, as Medbh McGuckian says, "we coiled / in the lifelong snake of sleep, we poised together // against the crevice formed by death's forefinger / and thumb, where her shoulder splits when desire / goes further than the sender will allow." [84] He woke us; we were given good news at the break of dawn. He would heal naturally – our baby. There was no brain bleed. He had a concussion. But I was painfully aware that like my sister and

my friend, we could have just as easily and quickly and unexpected-
ly received terrible news. It happens every day. And either way, we
would have only had the hospital corridors to wander in search (or
not) of the divine. Either way, we would have walked blindly through
the night. And either way, the prayers would have been in the sheer
wakefulness, the fear, the worry and even the numbness.

Buckled Under the Weight of the Spring Sky

The babe's bruised arms, pale
daffodil petals on white sheets.

I do not want to let him sleep
on sheets crisped with pain

so I carry him into the hallway's
creases while the panic of children

ricochets off every clean white
right angle. At home the clothes

are piled high like the last
melting snowflakes layered

with grime and stench and city.
Since he had the first seizure,

there have been two electrical
storms. It is finally night; we are

alone trembling for doctor's
words. This test is the weight

of the dark winter sky. Across
the East River, water pools

like blood on the bathroom
floor where my firstborn secretly

pours it out of the bath while
my husband is not looking.

I breathe into the babe's hair,
twist curls around fate reckoned

with since he was born. Forgive
me—I thought—we were here

when another boy I loved wrestled
with tubes and veins and breath

and lost. The bee sting smell
of this hospital is the same.

In the last few hours, the mold
in the window frames at home

has become a pressing matter.
I pace out every mother's worry—

those (my sister) who were pinned
(forever) into hospital corners

where children bleat under long
rungs of fluorescent lights. The babe

wakes from needled dreams when
the doctor comes in to say go home

to your overturned life, to dishes
fragmented across wooden floors.

What did it mean to be a mystic that night? It didn't mean an experience or awareness of the divine. No, it was simpler than that – as simple as pacing the wing of the hospital all through the night, pulling the IV stand along with us. What did it mean to pray but to move my body to soothe him, to offer my skin as a solace, to walk the maze of the hospital with my weary steps, waiting and wondering.

Mysticism is possible whether or not I felt the divine through the night (I did not). I was part of the divine even as I was decreated and disrupted to such an extent that I was thinned out, made transparent, loosened at the seams and diving deep within my skin trying to hold onto some semblance of sanity and survive. The walls around me fell down and I was undone into the heart of God, whether or not I could feel God.

Could it be that though I did not see or experience God, that closing my eyes as Silas was poked with that needle again and again was my clinging to the divine? God was the desolation within me as I tried to block out my son's pain. God was my hands in his hair, on his skin – trying to soothe. God was the way that everything became so transparent – who and what mattered, who I loved, what it means to love nakedly and fervently in this wild world. God is not veiled behind authorities. Experience, rather, is the mother of any true-hearted mysticism. We are never further or closer to the divine than we are right now. And right now, I am blessedly home from the hospital.

Courage

*Don't say, don't say there is no water
to solace the dryness at our hearts.*

— Denise Levertov[85]

Slowly but surely, we have been recovering from our night in the hospital and the surrounding fear. Yesterday, I found my thoughts back there, back in the waiting, back in the CT scan room when they gave Silas the shot to make him still and it ran through his body like a seizure, reminding me of the unknowns that are always present. It took my breath away, just the memory. Tears stung my eyes and my hands went to my stomach where I felt like I had been kicked. In the last month, we took Jude to the hospital for croup (he recovered quickly after receiving steroids) and Silas to the hospital for the concussion. Days later we all got the stomach flu. The flu has interrupted our sleep and Silas wakes a few times a night with a leaking and explosive diaper. We are exhausted and discouraged.

But because life doesn't wait for you to be well-rested, and I cannot even imagine that day, we have begun to talk seriously about the possibility of leaving New York City for Flagstaff, Arizona – where no full-time job for Aaron awaits but where we have family and some history and where Jude says he wants to live because of the deer and the space. As we have mulled this over, we have weighed the great gains and the incredible risks. It's such a huge risk that it actually makes me feel lightheaded.

I cannot help but think about how every morning, Jude takes the tiniest handful of birdseed out to the sidewalk. He does not want the birds to go hungry. It is late winter and there is little left to forage. But the birds will starve on his stingy offering. He thinks his prudence is saving them, but this is when excess is called for, which I fear he cannot learn from me.

Aaron has had more imagination around moving back to Flagstaff recently than ever before and there is a part of me that wants to ride that wave. I said this to him last night. But I am afraid, which is why, in the midst of this conversation that contains my wildest dreams, I have spearheaded an effort to find a new home in Croton-on-Hudson. You might be shaking your head.

As soon as I showed some restraint, he said that while he does have a new energy toward imagining a different life and hopes he will be able to choose Flagstaff someday, he would also like to have the chance to internalize this shift and move more gently in this direction. He feels like buying the house in Croton gives him that time and he hopes that maybe when we are ready to move to Flagstaff it will feel less like jumping off a cliff. I wonder if I lost my chance to my own fear.

But either way, Croton is where our heads tell us to go, even though our hearts may be urging us to do otherwise. We have come up empty-handed through all the job inquiries and applications. And I don't feel like I can wait another year to decide. I want Jude to start school next year in the place we have chosen to call home. Right now, Croton is the only way forward we can really imagine following through on. There is another future, maybe even a better one, but it seems too risky and out of reach.

We found another house. It is quite old but sweet and fairy-tale like with a curved steep roof, a rounded front door, a built-in breakfast nook and a large and long backyard with an enclosed garden and a view of the Hudson way off in the distance. It sounds like a dream when I write it down. When we entered it, it felt like a possibility. And it also felt like a stretch for our hearts and our finances. But even so, we feel like we are desperate for a change and quickly, so we put an offer down; it was accepted. It is the third house we have put an offer on in Croton-on-Hudson. And tomorrow we put earnest money down. I keep telling myself that in this situation there is no perfect decision and that no decision is forever. I tell myself that this is safer this way. It is scary, but it isn't as scary as going to Flagstaff. It isn't jumping off that cliff.

I have prayed in the more traditional way more in the last week than I have in a very long time. And in that prayer, I feel like I am supposed to move from my head into my heart, but I'm incredibly resistant. Richard Rohr says that prayer is a movement toward being able to say *yes*. But yes to what? If nothing else, I suppose that engaging in the passionate process of discernment is more significant than whether or not the decision turns out to be "right." At least, I am trying to believe that.

This morning I rode the Seven Train to Manhattan to visit Vivienne again and likely for one of the last times. She knows my deep longing to move to the forest. She knows that if I could move anywhere, I would move back to Flagstaff, Arizona. She knows that I quickly jump to asking, "Who gets exactly what they want? Why should I expect that?" She knows that I don't want to ask Aaron to leave his career or his job. She knows too much sometimes.

Even knowing all of these things, she asks me to close my eyes and imagine a road that leads to Flagstaff and a road that leads to Croton-on-Hudson. In the sanctuary of my heart, these roads are clear and sunlit. I stand where the roads meet and from there diverge and look down the road to Flagstaff with physical longing. I want to take that road. I think that it may even be the *right* road, whatever that means, but even in the silence and privacy of my own heart, I know I cannot choose that path.

As I stand there, it seems like courage is asking me to reach for Flagstaff but that just doesn't feel possible. I am human and imperfect and sometimes I am more fearful than I am brave. Life is messy. Mysticism is messy. Marriage is messy. This is what I tell myself, standing there. And so, I choose to take the road that leads to

Croton-on-Hudson. As far as I'm concerned, we will put our earnest money down tomorrow and hope for the best.

As I walk out of Vivienne's four-story walkup that looks out over Washington Park, I pray for something like forgiveness for my lack of courage. Despite the call of the mountains and forests, despite a knowing, I simply cannot succumb to that desire. As I ride the Seven Train back to Sunnyside, my decision to put money down on the house in Croton feels like failure. I cannot explain it. After all, I am trying to protect a marriage and a family. It is not a joyful decision; it is a resigned one. There is not a complete absence of hope in this decision – not at all. But there is some sadness that I do not feel like I have the courage to ask Aaron for what might be the better way. There is some sadness because what if my desires are important for our family as a whole and I just cannot see that?

But I am so afraid of Aaron sinking into depression and anger without a job he loves. *God be with me,* I ask, *even in my fear, especially in my fear.* Today, I cannot make a better decision and by morning the decision is due. Purchasing this home in Croton enfolds some of my desires for more quiet, with some of Aaron's. We cannot have it all, I remind myself. And my prayer is that this decision to put down roots is one that will be healing for us, will lead me out of this long sense of exile, and will allow us to sink even deeper into our life and love and family. That seems noble enough, if I can't have courage.

Pleasure

We are made up of layers, cells, constellations.

— Anaïs Nin [86]

Last night, Aaron poured two glasses of red wine. We sat down on the big brown couch that takes up half our living room to make our final decision about the earnest money for the home in Croton-on-Hudson. I did not tell Aaron about my process or about my meeting with Vivienne. I simply said that I felt like it was a reasonable decision to go ahead with the house purchase even though we both feel concerned about the finances and the commute and whether or not I will be happy there long term.

Aaron did not seem as sure, which surprised me. He talked about how the bold and courageous move is Flagstaff, but he is also afraid and doesn't want to be impulsive. We were quiet for a long time. And then I asked him if he wanted me to lead him in a practice that I had done with Vivienne around this same question. He said yes. The lights were low. A beeswax candle in a small pewter dish flickered between us, its light absorbed into the glow of crimson wine. The streetlights shone brightly into our front window. There was the distant sound of a car alarm – always a car alarm.

Aaron closed his eyes and I guided him with a few simple words to that fork in the road. I said that there were two ways before him – one to Croton-on-Hudson and one to Flagstaff. I described Croton-on-Hudson as a small river town with parks and rolling hills and brilliant leaves in autumn and a commuter train to Aaron's job in Queens. I said that the Flagstaff road led to a small mountain town near family (his and mine), brilliant aspen leaves in autumn, trails to wander and no certain future in philosophy. I paused to give Aaron time to look down each path before proceeding. He opened his eyes and said, "When I go to the deepest place within, there are not two roads. There is only one road. And it leads to Flagstaff."

I was speechless. I still am.

And so I was finally able to say yes. I thought again of prayer being the ability to say yes. [87] I thought of all my circling around the holiness of desire and the instincts and deep knowing of the body. I thought about stars and the scent of ponderosas. And to all of that, I said yes.

Aaron called our realtor this morning and told her we would not be purchasing the house. It felt painfully real to let that house go. But we had to do it. It was nothing short of a miracle that our hearts were in the same place at the same time. This is not something we can take for granted in our marriage.

I called a few family members and dear friends and told them we would be moving to Flagstaff. There were gasps and tears of joy. There are just as many gasps and tears of grief for and with those we are leaving behind, and for what we were leaving behind.

We went on a walk and Aaron said that even if it doesn't work out and even if we eventually leave Flagstaff, he knows it is what we should do. He knows that it is worth it. He knows that we need to make this step, take this risk and surrender to it.

Aaron is moving to Flagstaff for my sake and because he wants a different life for himself and for our family – something other than commuter trains and long work hours, something other than car alarms as an evening serenade. He too longs for some wildness and calm places to roam for our boys, less financial strain, living near family, a more quiet and generous existence. He longs for something simpler. But he is also listening to the deep desires of my heart to make a home in a place I already belong. He knows how much I don't want to begin again yet again. He is risking his own deep desires as I have done before him. It is brave. It is beautiful. It is terrifying. And I know what I have always known – that for me and in so many ways, it is easier to give than to receive.

At the same time, I am terrifyingly happy. All I can think of is the family we will be received by, the quiet, the sky and trees and forests, the song of the quaking aspens, the mountain I have missed so much it has hurt.

Mysticism was lived out in a place of sacrifice for many years – traipsing around city after city following Aaron's calling and dream. And now mysticism leads me to the center of my heart where deep desire is born. I was able to speak out those desires, to be connected to them, but I wasn't able, finally, to choose them for myself. Aaron was able to hear those desires and move toward the center of that potential joy. And I think that is the mysticism of marriage, in particular. Sometimes we choose what the other person needs, as Aaron did for me. Sometimes we give what we most need, as I did for Aaron. And this time that gift came back around. That is not always the case, but I am grateful that it is today.

It is not simple. It never has been for us. And it probably won't be in the next few years, either. But whatever has come before and whatever lies ahead, I can say yes to it – whether it be carved by pain or etched with pleasure. I know it will likely be both, just like the past. And tonight, I can see that there is a path of mysticism through the landscape of my life – a path that leads me home.

I have been thinking about how my body feels like a different body when I am in Flagstaff. There are small things like my hair is a different texture. My skin is brighter (and drier) and my freckles stand out. My breaths are deeper. Movement feels easier. I feel more inexplicably lithe. And today when I woke up, I held reminiscences of those feelings in my limbs and skin and lungs and smiled. After so many years of sacrifice and of being out of place, I am astonished to be moving to a place I already call home, a place I will not have to start over.

Despite my concerns (and I still have many) over Aaron's wellbeing in Flagstaff, I am in the midst of a free-fall into a dream I have barely dared to harbor in my entire adulthood. This homegoing is one of sweetness, pleasure, relief and deep joy. This beauty is another way to encounter the divine – albeit a way I am less familiar with. But I know this encounter will be mostly in the wilderness of my skin. And here I was thinking that I was destined to chronicle the mysticism of the shadows alone.

I'm surprised at how much this communion is centered around the body. And then I'm not surprised at all. Body and soul are temples for communion, icons of the divine incarnate, prism points where light is refracted further. Truth is often distilled by the body. *We* are places of worship. We do not have to go elsewhere. Today I abide with the divine as I imagine into a life I have longed for by allowing myself to anticipate the pleasure that moving there evokes as mystical. It is not surprising that there is some resistance because pleasure (especially physical pleasure) has been historically relegated outside the realms of religion. This is blessedly pushing my limits of what it means to be a mystic. But if the Mystery can be known in the shadows, the Mystery can also be known in the light. But I think again of what Vivienne said about how there is a mysticism of lights up and lights down. And both are equally bewildering.

I am filled with imagining a slower and more deliberate way of life, one that includes stars and more stars, deer tracks in the snow, family stopping by unannounced, mountains to climb, a small steady community, fields of wildflowers, sunsets to behold with open arms. We will finally see the horizon.

I came across this poem today, which I wrote a few months ago before I dared to imagine that we would ever choose Flagstaff. It always astonishes me what our hearts know before our minds can understand.

Prayer

That the days will lengthen like threads
pulled from wool sweaters until my skin
is next to sky. That we will assemble

our latticed place in the world. That
we will be kind. That our weft and warp
won't bar the windows. That I will never

forget the warmth of four morning-bodies
mortared into one small bed. That we
will uncover the old trail that leads us home.

That home will be forests and generosity.

I can see now that I have turned over the tables of my original understanding of God. I can begin to accept desire and the satisfaction of that desire as a portal to the Mystery and to a mystical way of being. I know now that I do not have to sink beneath the ocean of desire, to disappear under the furious waves, curled tight, breath held. I do not have to pretend that I do not want a clearing in the forest, old trees for new friends so much so that I cannot sleep at night. I do not have to put my heart on lockdown.

We reach the soul by way of the body, try as we might to circumvent it. Joanna Macy says that the body is what anchors us to our mutual belonging. And in that mutual belonging there is suffering yes, but also, and today, pleasure and satiation. I do not think it accidental that a mysticism of pleasure had to first undergo a reclamation of the body. I had to first see matter (and my body) as holy. This is what that reclamation was preparing me for.

It is not just Flagstaff that has brought me joy. But it is this particular joy that is one of my entrances to a mysticism of pleasure. And in making my way into this new open field, I experience the joy of every day differently. I experience it as prayer – the nurturing and loving the bodies of my children and husband. Silas knows the wonder of sensuality and pleasure better than most. He is all smiles and cuddles these days. This morning, when I kissed him over and over again upon wakening, he closed his eyes and his exhale was tremulous with pleasure that quickly became mine. The look on his face was one of such contentment that I caught my breath. In the wake of his joy, I allow myself to get lost in the sensual intensity of imagining Flagstaff as home. This is today's act of surrender to a single dream. This is today's abiding in the heart of mysticism. And I ask for the courage to stay in the pleasure, to not turn my back.

Community

Let the soul of a man take the whole universe for its body.

— Simone Weil[88]

Although I have stayed primarily in the realm of the personal, mysticism has a bearing on the world. Experiences of the divine are meant to be shared. They are not solely for the sake of the individual. I do not mean that all experiences of the divine need to be chronicled or spoken aloud (though I imagine some of them certainly do). That said, these experiences create or decreate something within us that both belongs to us and never did to begin with. If the heart of mysticism is belovedness, then it is concerned with the wellbeing of the entire community of beings. It is concerned with the day-to-day. It is concerned for justice and equality. It is concerned for suffering and hunger, violence and despair. Sometimes it feels impossible to know how to address all that needs repair. But if we begin in the muddy terrain of our own lives, then at least we begin, and there are ever widening circles from there.

Before we celebrate or bless or create something in our house, I try to remind my boys (and myself) that every vision, prayer or act is for the entire community of beings, even if we cannot yet see how. When we experience the divine in and through pleasure – the pleasure of the sand beneath our feet, the pleasure of the wind upon our faces, the nostalgia evoked in a piece of art, the soaring of our hearts through music – it is meant to reach beyond us and it often does, effortlessly, in the simple act of sharing. When we experience the divine when we are lost and up a creek, when we are adrift and blinded by pain, we are joined with others who suffer. When we experience the love of God, we are given the chance to love more freely. When we feel the Living Wind, we know it is also touching others.

I abide less in the realm of universalism and more in the realm of mutual belonging. The tradition in which I was raised focused on salvation as an act of God on behalf of an individual. And similarly, individuals could only seek salvation for themselves alone. But my experience of salvation is much different. It is collective and communal. It is participatory. We are a part of one another. We belong to one another. Suffering, joy, mercy and love touch the collective even when they feel completely private or when they seem to belong to someone else.

Mysticism is in part about bearing witness to suffering and pain. There is the internal witness of mysticism that a dear friend brought to my attention when she once said that dreams are a witness to the soul. That rings true for me – that within the heart of mysticism, we can be witnessed even when we are profoundly alone and even when we are blessedly asleep. And there is the external witness that is stoked by mysticism – that doesn't close its eyes to the violence in the world and that knows how to scream for help or in protest when necessary. I want my prayers to be actions that reckon with the sinister spirits of injustice and suffering both on a macro and micro level. And I want my actions to be prayers.

Angeles Arrien says that we are to "walk the mystical path with practical feet."[89] I think that this can mean so many things. But in part I think it means that we continue to ask the question *why* when suffering is happening, even though there will never be a satisfactory answer and even when we cannot solve the problem. Questions emerge from an experience of death or impasse or despair – though I do not claim that this makes it worthwhile. You will have your own, as I have mine. I want to be brave enough to keep asking these questions. *How long must I remain at this place of impasse, circling it, and looking for a way in? How can I remain human? Why does it seem like I'm expected to walk through a stone wall? When can sit down, lean back and rest?*

I want mysticism to follow me into every inlet, into all the cracks and crumbles. I want to walk a muddy path of mysticism even when I give up completely. And sometimes I do, for a time. I want mysticism to be able to hold me when I'm ready to fight again. There is still so much to fight for.

Teilhard de Chardin says that "we make our own soul throughout all our earthly days; and at the same time we collaborate in another work, another opus, which infinitely transcends, while at the same time it narrowly determines, the perspectives of our individual achievement: the completing of the world." [90] There is still so much to complete – in my own life and in the world. When I see this incompleteness of the world in the unjust systems, in the suffering of a child, in the traumas that many of my residents in Armenia have borne, I am filled with longing.

Longing is a weight on my back. And it is the water beneath me, holding me up. It keeps me up at night. It keeps me from moving too quickly or far. It holds me down. The longing itself is the Mystery within and Mystery without, God in my soul, the soul of the world. God of clay and muck and heavens and earth and all of this – the divine milieu. God as the One that is roots, groping the earth, entwining my soul. God as piercing. Sometimes the divine longing sends me dancing like a dervish in the rain of all that has dissolved around me. In Beverly Lanzetta's *Hymn to Hagia Sophia,* she prays: "Life is nothing more than a longful dialog with you." I hunger and pine for what I can never have in its entirety because I hunger and pine for the completion of the world.

This sacred longing is not indicative of a lack or deficit on either my part or on the part of the Mystery as I once imagined. But it is part of the larger opus. It is part of the completion of the world. Longing is how the world and my soul will be transformed.

In the mystical life, there are times we move in and out of the shadows, behind buildings or mountains or clouds. I, for one, traipse the earth wounded, healed, fallen, broken, lifted up. I am emptied and then full. I am a crescent – waxing and waning. I vacillate between the mysticism of lights up and lights down.

My longing for the sacred is threaded through the tapestries of life and death. It sings in the minerals close to the earth's core, alights on the ribbons of dawn, circles around my wanderings. The weight of that longing has driven me to conduct long dances and solo walks through the city. It drives me underground. It finds me on bluffs overlooking the sea. It propels me to dive deep into books (too many books). It makes me soar across the seas to Armenia time and time again even when I'm weary. It keeps me from sleep. It keeps me from moving too quickly. It keeps me tied down. The weight of longing is my constant companion.

I long for it all. I want the lost hymns. I want every angle and petal of every flower and weed of this life, even and especially those that still lie dormant underground. Portions and petals, like scraps of moonlight, have fallen like the Mystery into my hands. The sightings of the moon and of the divine, however brief and fleeting, make up a life. These moments, however small, we name blessed.

Epilogue: Storm

I have occasionally described my standpoint to my friends as "the narrow ridge." I wanted by this to express that I did not rest on the broad upland of a system that includes a series of sure statements about the absolute, but on a narrow, rocky ridge between the gulfs, where there is only certainty of meeting what remains undisclosed.

— Martin Buber [91]

I have wondered at times if this book feels impossible to close because life does not often provide a sense of closure – because it is more cyclical than linear. There is always another reckoning and there will be more of the same – often with only a slight variation of theme. But while all that is true, while we all spiral through light into dark, love into hate, longing into despair, birth into death, and back again, I think it feels impossible to close because you need to know what came next.

The last few months in New York City disappeared behind the gauze of change. All I remember now are the questions. *What will be left of me when the world stops spinning and finally there is quiet in a forest of pines?*

I remember questions like this. And I remember the goodbyes, which I resisted – wanting to leave without a trace before sunrise, only because it is impossible to wrap up a life in a hug and a promise. I didn't know how to make the ends meet – the ends of one city to a beloved town, the ends of one garden to an acreage, the hands of one friend to another's. But I weathered them anyhow and said goodbye to the beloved sycamores, to Aaron's long-sought job, to walking everywhere, to my neighbors, to the people who had cared for my children, to my dear friend-at-first sight and her beloved family and to all those we had grown to love, to a siren-street, to claret, to juneberry blossoms, and to the only geography in which we had known what it means to be a parent.

And after the goodbyes, we left. But it was one ugly surrender. We packed our belongings into boxes: the books, generosity, plates, resentment, spices, and security. After sorting out the knots of hand-spun yarn my cousin had given me, after emptying the house, lining our life up roadside, we learned that the truck was too small to hold all that. (I should have known that resentment would take up too much space.)

There was a tropical storm brewing and rain threatened to hammer us down, so we stacked our losses at the curb (rocking chair, vacuum, tricycle, dresser, rug, broom) to watch the ruining. The bones of our years grew soaked and shabby before our eyes. I had to keep telling myself they were only possessions – that losing to rain did not mean we could not carry our life a country's width west. I had to remind myself that we chose this leaving after years upon years that ask questions. And this, the year, had answered.

But I didn't expect the answer to be a storm.

As the orange velvet chair wilted in the rain, the heavens gaped open and we stood drowning. When we tried to put the car on the trailer behind the moving van, we realized the trailer was broken. We called for a replacement only to hear a recorded message: *closed for a long holiday weekend.* We were taking up the whole road in the dark with our U-haul, our goodbyes, broken lamps, looming flights and Aaron's frustration something physical between us.

We stood in the rain wrangling with a broken trailer instead of wandering through our empty home saying goodbye, remembering streamers, turkeys, solstice dances, summer fires, cracked-open windows, the floor that creaked where Silas was born, and rooms that contained spools of sleep and dreams. Our well-laid plan was to slip the last key through the mail slot and walk away together. We had planned to wave goodbye as Aaron drove off to clean stretches of highway and the boys and I hopped in a taxi to catch our plane. We had planned to meet five days later in Arizona.

But our flight was soon leaving and the trailer was irreparable and each raindrop dented our skin as Aaron dissolved on the wet concrete in a rage. Eventually, I had to leave but with the sour taste of his anger in my mouth. I'm not saying I can blame him. I'm not saying I haven't had those moments myself. I'm just saying that it wasn't what we expected.

The boys and I hailed our taxi and flailed through sheets of rain. Jude was chanting his goodbyes: Sylvan, hydrangeas, subways, Daddy. I told myself Aaron would follow after the skies were clear, the trailer replaced and his own lonely farewell to the empty echoes of what used to be our home. Jude asked why his tricycle was left on the sidewalk and I told him that sometimes storms take more than what has already been taken.

I tried to rise above the storm (and make our flight). I tried to submit to the fierce baptism of leaving. Is this what it always feels like to walk away from a life that has run its course? Whatever the answer, this definitely wasn't what I thought the final iteration of my seventeen-year exile would be. I didn't know the threads would fray so thin. And I didn't yet know that they would soon snap.

As soon as our flight landed in Arizona, my sister went into labor. Bedraggled and rain-splattered, I rushed to the hospital, this time to watch her son Will come into the world, shattering our hearts with his breath and beauty. By the time I pulled into the driveway of my mother's house, my childhood home, I was entirely spent from beauty and loss. And I didn't even know what was to come – that our homecoming would be like the spiral fracture of the toe I broke on one of my last days in Queens. It was not an easy leaving. It was not an easy landing. There were storms on both ends.

The stars hid every night that first week, balking at my hubris in presuming I could banish exile. Within a few days of our return, while Aaron was still driving the moving truck across the country, lightning struck a huge ponderosa twenty feet from my childhood home. The aged ponderosa that had sheltered me through childhood, adolescence and adulthood grappled with the claws of electricity and lost. Wood shards flew through the air singed with fire. The heartwood broke open and the air was laced with sap. After the storm passed, we walked outside to survey the tree's damage – another spiral fracture. Now there were two.

The homecoming did not offer tidy closure to a long and untidy journey. It got muddier and then muddier still. I have wondered many times if I returned home only to split open on blessedly familiar ground. With my return home, there was a turnstile violence of old familial pain which surfaced and stung. After Aaron left a job he loved, he floundered for purpose and then sank like metal in a murky pond. He didn't know how to come up for air. His increasing anger was our collective undoing and none of us came out unscathed. So he and I separated for a time and then came back together. Somewhere in the middle of it all, Julian was born. He was a shock of tenderness on our thread-bare and unraveling hearts.

Broken Open,   There's Always More

(The day I ask my husband to leave,
—to take some solitude, I tell the three boys—)

we bend down to see   scarce   wool-moss shining on stone

(to heal (or fail) old injuries
that transmute into anger.)

Our feet are bare and heavy   on cold earth. We trace the pale
of winter along limbs changed   by months of layers and loss

and the way the body silently   mends itself after birth—
but not all the way,   not the diastasis recti, the gap

(I've all but given up).

Here is my soft   spot   where intestines push out,
form a long ridge that weakens me   through and though he does not
know that

(broken),

there's always more.

(He is an ice storm that cracks the roof to ruin—
his anger, a hardening yolk.)

Three hens died mid-   winter when prey were

meager.

The children stoop to gather   the first two eggs in
winter-chafed   hands.
They are fragile   stones in our palms.
One drops.
They are warm weights   pulled from underground,
tipped by the scales   of equinox.

We will save a few for Easter   far away though it may seem.

The baby's hands river along   my bare arms as he rediscovers
my skin after I shed sweaters, as if he did not once inhabit me

        (as I came to know the cost of anger caging us in.).

One pale egg broke over the hot   cast iron pan.

                (One, we are missing.)

Fragility mends only by breaking   open.
And diastasis, put another way   more than two fingers' width
of separation—

                (he has (not (yet) to) split open.).

One Lenten rosebud pushes   through pine needles,
                (tight-fisted,)   swollen.

The boys sift through hand-me-downs,

        (thinking there is not enough to go around).

It's Spring, they   (shout.)   We're new.

                (Look here,)

Mama. We're new.   Daddy will like this one,
once he's done   with
                (solitude.).

He told us he is working hard to

        (love us even more.).

Mama, do you know the secret   about love?
Madrinha told us   on that long snowy walk
after Daddy got so angry.   They whisper:

        (There's always more.).

Aaron and I went to a lot of counseling to try to stitch our family and our hearts back together again after all the storms. We had our share of come-to-Jesus conversations – deep reckonings about whether or not we could make this marriage (and life in Flagstaff) work. Simultaneously, I came close to burnout in my work as an activist in Armenia. I attempted to take a remedial sabbatical. In all of this, in marriage and vocation and mothering and mysticism, I learned that we are not called to do what we wish were possible. We are called to do what is possible.

All my poems filled up with fissures and fault lines. I had thought they would be lit up by stars. Eventually Aaron got another job in philosophy but now that too is threatened by pandemic-related university layoffs. We do not (ever) know what is next. We do not know what joy and pain lie in wait either under the surface or beyond the horizon.

But in spite of it all, we made a home in a cedar shake shingle house with a back deck that allows us to sleep under the stars most nights during the summer. We sleep five in a row, our feet near the weak spot in the roof where ice dams form each winter. Our breaths are a slipknot some nights around carefully harvested peace, some nights around the dredges of fear. Every once in a while, I wake to a deer's tentative steps. The crescent moon haunts the sky and lays claim over the children's twig-boned bodies that I love so loosely.

In this house, we have had feasts and fury both. I stir soup now to warblers *and* whines, to hands hooked through my legs and glasses of musty wine. I still light the candle every night before our meal and the children do their best to extinguish it before we are even done with the simple song: *Dear God, thank you for this food. Thank you, rain and bees. Thank you, sun and moon. Thank you, Holy Mystery.* There is so much more to thank but we start here. There is a pile of worn-out shoes by the front and back doors. There are always oats scattered on the floor from breakfast.

Tonight, when the flies swarmed around the dinner table and Julian was afraid, he cried out, "Brave, Mama, Brave" as if the incantation alone would be sufficient to abate his fear. It is my incantation as well. I love how he only uses the word *brave* when he is afraid. I suppose that's the only time we need it.

How Fires are Started or the Impossibility of Embodied Silence

I wayside the garden. The first frost should crochet
us tonight. I pull the last of the tomatillos, putter,
plunk old scraps of steel on the side of the house—

       make a messy pile, yet another mess.

Under one damp log are piles of slug eggs,
transparent and perfect. The middling collects
and waylays them. They stick together, stick to everything.

Later, while nursing the babe, I feel egg sac
film on my hands. I read the same two sentences
over and over and over. [92]

       I want to consider immanence and transcendence

but not as discrete concepts. Rather, I want to explore overlap
and saturation. *Tucked into the binding of my unfinished*
book are sight words. I review them with my firstborn over

       and overlap and over: once, does, only, two.
I talk to the psychologist.   *I worry.*
The middling asks when the baby slugs will be born.
It's hard to say never when we have been the flint

and steel of their death. It's hard to say never
after I ruined the children's day, made a transcendent mess
when the butter dish slipped from my hand.

       I felt the tumble, the slight blunder.

I watched it fall, spark on the floor, too many pieces
to mend, ceramic shards pointing out of the butter mound

                    like cloves in oranges, good for nothing.
It's embarrassing but I cried thunderstorms.
Why can't I keep anything beautiful? *Or maybe it was*

I break everything beautiful. *Either way, I couldn't stop*

and the boys tried to saturate my embodied flames.
We can find you a new one that is old. *You have us.*
Where did you find this one?

            In the far corridors of the East Village,

near where my first baby (I point) was born. He slept
at home while I made gorgeously lonely with the streets.
It's a five-day drive from slug eggs and tomatillo husks.

At the thunder, I stepped down into a clay-crowded potter's shop.
            Excuse me, Mama, but when
will the baby slugs be born?
My grandma (I haven't called her back all week)

used to send Christmas money before the saturation
of Alzheimer's and I traded it in for
earth. It was early motherhood.
The practical and mystical were just starting to overlap,

            one the flint, one the spark.

I have tried to stay with the places that require bravery – the practical, the messy, the trivial, loss and the long nights. And when I have strayed from these places, I have returned quickly, chided by my own crafty methods and means of escape. I have followed the Mystery through cyclical motions, through wind that lifts fast into the sky, and then settles back down again. I have listened to the roar and whispers of the divine through earth, city, body, family, marriage and the work of my hands because it is from this skin and station in life that I love and serve the Mystery, along with the collective.

I am already a different person than when I started this book. I am certain that is always the case. My view of mysticism is wider, deeper, ever still. That is the beauty of life. It asks and beckons us to a place of articulation only to shatter that very articulation into a thousand pieces. Then, we pick up those pieces and make another mosaic that will break again and again. So, I dare to place these words and phrases and poems into your hands, not because it is my final word, but because it is a word, a simple word that I harvested from the seabed of my own life, from the dregs. And in my wildest prayers, it will be a word that spurs you toward your own articulation, your own mosaic. May it be so.

Acknowledgments

What shall we sing, while the fire burns down?
We can sing only specifics, time's rambling tune,
the places we have seen, the faces we
have known. I will sing you...

— Annie Dillard [93]

So many times I have built a spiritual home out of mud, rain, rocks, and clay only to tear it down because a stone was not in the right place. So many times, I started all over again, dirty and exhausted. Thank you to those of you who stood by and watched with eyes of love and acceptance, who asked open-hearted questions until I could begin to articulate what I was trying to create, who waited patiently until I was ready to invite you in and when I finally did, sat in my make-shift shelter and called it blessed.

In the crafting of this book, I relied on so many generous readers (and souls). Lucy Pearce and Womancraft Publishing, thank you for believing in this book and for bringing it into the world. Gretchen Hampshire, thank you for reading the first few chapters of this book in its inception and assuring me that it had a place in the world (and in your heart). Kelley Ward, thank you for your edits and for walking with me as we both wove our own unique tapestries of feminine spirituality. Emily Neuman Bauerle, thank you for your insights and for letting these words (and me) accompany you through the shadows. Chris Crew, thank you all your poetry edits and for coming up with *Shit Creek Mysticism*. I still wonder if that should have been the title of the book. Vanya, thank you for unraveling these ideas with me over the last two decades and for loving this book from start to finish. You made sure it found its way into the world. For your insights, edits and support, thank you to Tamie Parker Song, Jill O'Brien, Shauna Bryant Yoder, Rachel Shuler and Katherine Larson.

I have also relied on so many generous souls as I have crafted my days. To those who made my time in New York City rich and meaningful: the Black-Rogers family – Jenn, Josh, Sylvan and Ember, Marinda Kaiser, Keeney, Jessica Wahlstrom, Hillit Zwick, Jessica Hunsdon, Dan Battey, and Jen Sauer. To those in Flagstaff who welcomed me back and helped me create a new home: Susan Barnes-Werley, Emily Neuman Bauerle, Jill Henkenius, Cassandra Hunsdon, Anna Neuman Singleton, Christopher Alexander, Terry Grantham, Isha Braun, Threshold Choir and the Freemotion community. To those whose love and friendship are now outside of geographical bounds but who tether my heart: Vanya Stier-Van Essen, Chris Crew, Kelley Ward, Rachel Shuler, Liz Cooksey, Gretchen Hampshire, Rachel Treadaway, Katherine Larson, Holly Hammond and Amy Lowe. To my spiritual directors: Vivienne Joyce, for your companionship and prayers while I was in New York City and to Mary Ellen Burton and Cathy Olds. To the ones I call beloved in Armenia, loving you has changed my heart, turned it blessedly inside-out and making it restless for still more change on behalf of all those who live on the margins, that the margins might be no more. To Bridget Brown, Juliet Setian and Alya Kirakosan, thank you for coming alongside of me in this work and for making it your own. You have accompanied me on a lonely road. And finally, to those who I remembered to include only after it was too late, thank you.

Family is where I was blessed to learn love and forgiveness. To my grandparents, Max and Thelma Biegert, for their steadfast love and presence. Shauna, thank you for your profound love, for the sweet gift of sisterhood, and for giving me your blessing to include the story of your beloved son, Weston Max, whose presence is still with me, whose absence is still a bruise on my heart. This may come as a surprise but I am not one to freely share my spiritual experiences with others. I hold them close in. I guard them fiercely. I had to fight so hard to make them my own that I have not wanted to put them back out into the world, both for fear that I might lose them and for fear that they might be cause for dissent. But thank you to my brother, Marcus, who beckoned me out of my silence with his fierce love and acceptance and asked me what that experience was. In that sharing over a cup of coffee, because of who you are and the way you listened, I realized I was ready to share this book with the world. Preston, thank you for your companionship and love on this ever-unfolding journey. I love the ways in which we diverge and are kindred. I love the magic we share. Thank you for your tenderness. To my mom, Rebecca, thank you for nurturing and honoring the contemplative in me as a young child. Thank you for always planning and treasuring time with just the two of us. Because of you, I have never known what it is to be completely alone or unloved. To my dad, Marshal Bryant, thank you for sharing your hunger and insatiable longing with me. I know that looks different for both of us, but it is a gift you gave to me. Because of you, I have never known what it is to be completely alone or unloved.

Finally, to the sweet and messy family that Aaron and I created through blood, sweat, tears and love. We are sustained by grace and fight both. Aaron, I love you and your huge, complicated heart. Thank you for trusting me to share parts of your story – even those parts that are still painful to the touch. Thank you for being the kind of person who thinks that the truth is worth telling. Thank you for the profound way you loved me when you let your dreams bow down to mine and up and moved to Flagstaff. Thank you to my boys – Jude Oliver, Silas Wendell and Julian Milo – for teaching this book to me day by day and night by night and for beckoning me into the realm of muddy mysticism, both literally and figuratively. I never imagined how much I could love you. You are my heart.

On the white page with infinite margins,
the space they measure is all incantation.

— St. John Perse[94]

Index

Endnotes

1. Marge Piercy. "To Be of Use".

2. Larry Levis. "Winter Stars".

3. Gregory Orr. *River Inside the River.*

4. Alexander Chee. *How to Unlearn Everything.*

5. Pierre Teilhard de Chardin. *The Divine Milieu.*

6. Evelyn Underhill in *Practical Mysticism* says, "Mysticism is the art of union with Reality."

7. Daniel Ladinsky. *A Year with Hafiz.*

8. Rebecca Solnit. *Recollections of my Nonexistence.*

9. Teresa of Avila. *Collected Works: The Book of Her Life.*

10. Simone Weil. *Forms of the Implicit Love of God.*

11. F.C. Happold. *Mysticism: A Study and Anthology.*

12. Simone Weil. *Gravity and Grace.*

13. Gerard Manley Hopkins. "On the Portrait of Two Beautiful Young People".

14. Joanna Macy. *The Great Turning.* "The assumption that selves are essentially separate, and thereby competitive, breeds insatiable wants. Hence the overriding goal of economic growth, to which our global system is increasingly addicted, and which is inherently suicidal."

15. Joanna Macy. *The Great Turning.*

16. Kim John Payne. *Simplicity Parenting.*

17. Layman P'ang was a Buddhist householder in the Zen tradition who lived from 740–808. This particular translation is taken from *The Enlightened Heart: An Anthology of Sacred Poetry* translated by Stephen Mitchell.

18. While I cannot find the reference any longer, I believe this question was asked by A.S. Byatt in *The Children's Book.*

19. Kathleen Norris. *Quotidian Mysteries.*

20. Fanny Howe. *Indivisible.*

21. Diane Di Prima. *The Mysteries of Vision: Some Notes on H.D.*

22. Elizabeth Robinson. "Gaps, Overflow and Linkage: A Synesthesiac Look at Motherhood and Writing", published in *The Grand Permission: new writings on poetics and motherhood.*

23. Pierre Teilhard de Chardin. *The Divine Milieu.*

24. Matins are morning prayers in the Anglican tradition.

25. Rainer Maria Rilke. *Fourth Duino Elegy.* Translated Joanna Macy.

26. William Kittredge. *The Nature of Generosity.*

27. *An Unexpected Wilderness: Christianity and the Natural World.* Edited by Carpenter, Colleen Mary.

28. Mary Oliver. "A Settlement".

29. Pierre Teilhard de Chardin. *The Divine Milieu.*

30. Abraham Joshua Heschel. *Man is Not Alone: A Philosophy of Religion.*

31. Jeremy Summerly. "Hildegard Von Bingen: Heavenly Revelations". Oxford Camerata.

32. Beverly Lanzetta. *A Radical Wisdom.*

33. Barbara Brown Taylor. *An Altar in the World.*

34. Pierre Teilhard de Chardin. *The Spiritual Power of Matter.*

35. Dorothee Soelle. *Strength of the Weak.*

36. Iris Marion Young. "Pregnant Embodiment" in *Throwing Like a Girl.*

37. Elizabeth Robinson speaks so eloquently on these matters in her essay "Gaps, Overflow, and Linkage: A Synethesiac Look at Motherhood and Writing".

38. Thomas Moore. *Care of the Soul: A Guide for Cultivating Depth and Sacredness in Everyday Life*

39. David Abrams. *The Spell of the Sensuous.*

40. *The Enlightened Heart: An Anthology of Sacred Poetry.* Translated by Stephen Mitchell.

41. Beverly Lanzetta. *A Radical Wisdom.*

42. David Abram. *Becoming Animal: An Earthly Cosmology.*

43. Many of these ideas are elaborated upon and fleshed out through Peter Levine's work, and especially within *In an Unspoken Voice: How the Body Releases Trauma and Restores Goodness.*

44. David Abram. *Becoming Animal: An Earthly Cosmology.*

45. Denise Levertov in "Variation and Reflection on a Theme by Rilke".

46. Barbara Brown Taylor. *An Altar in the World.*

47. Cynthia Borgeault. *Wisdom Way of Knowing.*

48. Mirabai Starr. *Wild Mercy.*

49. Jack Spicer in *After Lorca.*

50. Monica Sjöö and Barbara Mor. *The Great Cosmic Mother: Rediscovering the Religion of the Earth.*

51. Fred Gustafson. *The Black Madonna.*

52. Bill Plotkin. *Soulcraft.*

53. Rebecca Solnit. *Recollections of my Nonexistence.*

54. Marion Woodman. *The Pregnant Virgin.*

55. Elaine Aron. *The Highly Sensitive Person.*

56. Barbara Ehrenreich. *Dancing in the Streets: A History of Collective Joy.*

57. *The Complete Mystical Works of Meister Eckhart.* Translated by Maurice O'C. Walshe.

58. Rainer Maria Rilke. *Book of Hours.*

59. Belden Lane. *The Solace of Fierce Landscapes.*

60. Kathleen Fischer. *Women at the Well.*

61. Wendell Berry. *Terrapin: Poems by Wendell Berry.*

62. Robert Frost. "The Secret Sits".

63. Christian Wiman. *My Bright Abyss.*

64. PICC stands for 'peripherally inserted central catheter.'

65. Elizabeth Robinson. "Gaps, Overflow, and Linkage: A Synethesiac Look at Motherhood and Writing".

66. Ursula LeGuin. *The Farthest Shore.*

67. Regina Sara Ryan. *Dangerous Prayers.*

68. Adélia Prado. *Ex-Voto: Poems.* Translated by Ellen Dore Watson.

69. T. S. Eliot. "East Coker".

70. Thomas Merton. *New Seeds of Contemplation. The Great Dance.*

71. Exodus 33:23. Hebrew and Christian Scriptures.

72. James Finley. *Meditation for Christians.*

73. Cedrus Monte. *At the Threshold of Psycho-Genesis / The Mournful Face of God.*

74. Matthew Fox. *Meditations with Meister Eckhart.*

75. Anne Carson. "The Art of Poetry, No. 88." *The Paris Review.*

76. Though apophatic theology is a distinctly Christian phrase, similar ideas can be found in other traditions. The Zen tradition speaks of something similar in *sunyata*, the Sufi tradition's *fana*, and, among others the Hindu theological expression of *nirguna* when referring to Brahman being without attributes.

77. Joanna Macy with Krista Tippett. *On Being.*

78. Simone Weil. *Gravity & Grace.*

79. Rainer Maria Rilke. "You, Darkness." Translated by David Whyte.

80. Percy Bysshe Shelley. *Prometheus Unbound.*

81. Marge Piercy. "Unlearning Not to Speak" in *To Be of Use.*

82. Belden Lane. *The Solace of Fierce Landscapes.*

83. Teresa of Avila. (Attributed to her but can't be found in her body of work.)

84. Medbh McGuckian. "Breaking the Blue" in *Marconi's Cottage.*

85. Denise Levertov. "The Fountain".

86. Anaïs Nin. *The Diary of Anaïs Nin,* Vol. 4: 1944-1947.

87. Adapted from Richard Rohr, "Today Is a Time for Mercy," December 10, 2015, https://cac.org/richard-rohr-on-mercy-mp3.

88. Simone Weil. *Gravity and Grace.*

89. Angeles Arrien. *The Tarot Handbook.*

90. Pierre Teilhard de Chardin. *The Divine Milieu.*

91. Martin Buber. *Between Man and Man.* Trans. by Ronald Gregor Smith.

92. Elizabeth Robinson. "Gaps, Overflow, and Linkage: A Synethesiac Look at Motherhood and Writing."

93. Annie Dillard. *Life on the Rocks.*

94. St. John Perse. *Oiseaux.* Translated from the French by Robert Fitzgerald.

About the Author

Natalie Bryant Rizzieri is a poet, writer, activist, mother and mystic. Her poetry has appeared in journals such as *Denver Quarterly, Pleaides, Terrain.org,* and *Crab Orchard Review.* She is the winner of the Hackney Literary Award. She is the founder and director of *Friends of Warm Hearth,* a movement of forever homes for abandoned Armenians with special needs. She spends her free time, at least in spring, digging for earthworms, watching for ravens and col-
lecting moss. She is making a home deep in the forest near Flagstaff, Arizona, with her husband and three sons. This is her first book.

Permissions

My thanks to the publications and award in which the following poems have appeared or been honored.

Denver Quarterly "What Makes Life Holy"

Hackney Literary Award and *Birmingham Arts Journal* "Studies of the Dark"

Permafrost "Buckled Under the Weight of the Spring Sky"

Pleiades "No Rhythm"

Sugar House Review "Exodus" and "Now I am ready to tell how bodies are changed into other bodies."

About Womancraft

Womancraft Publishing was founded on the revolution-
ary vision that women and words can change the world.
We act as midwife to transformational women's words that have the
power to challenge, inspire, heal and speak to the silenced aspects of
ourselves.

We believe that:

> books are a fabulous way of transmitting powerful transformation,

> values should be juicy actions, lived out,

> ethical business is a key way to contribute to conscious change.

At the heart of our Womancraft philosophy is fairness and integ-
rity. Creatives and women have always been underpaid. Not on our
watch! We split royalties 50:50 with our authors. We work on a full
circle model of giving and receiving: reaching backwards, supporting
TreeSisters' reforestation projects, and forwards via Worldreader, pro-
viding books at no cost to education projects for girls and women.

We are proud that Womancraft is walking its talk and engaging so
many women each year via our books and online. Join the revolution!
Sign up to the mailing list at womancraftpublishing.com and find us
on social media for exclusive offers:

(f) womancraftpublishing

(y) womancraftbooks

(c) womancraft_publishing

**Signed copies of all titles available from
shop.womancraftpublishing.com**

About the Artist

Tara Turner, creator of the cover image 'Holding in Gold', is a self-taught digital artist and photographer who lives in the Similkameen Valley in British Columbia, Canada. Her digital artworks are inspired by the colours of changing seasons and the magical energy flow of the forest. She spends her free time roaming the moun-  tains and along the banks of the Similkameen River, where she creates artworks from fallen leaves, driftwood, wild flowers and river stones.

tara-turner.pixels.com

Wild & Wise:
sacred feminine meditations for
women's circles and personal awakening

Amy Bammel Wilding

The stunning debut by Amy Bammel Wilding is
not merely a collection of guided meditations, but
a potent tool for personal and global transforma-
tion. The meditations beckon you to explore the powerful realm of
symbolism and archetypes, inviting you to access your wild and wise
inner knowing.

Suitable for reflective reading or to facilitate healing and empow-
erment for women who gather in red tents, moon lodges, women's
circles and ceremonies.

> *This rich resource is an answer to "what can we do to go
> deeper?" that many in circles want to know.*
> **Jean Shinoda Bolen, MD**

Sisters of the Solstice Moon
(Book 1 of the When She Wakes series)

Gina Martin

On the Winter Solstice, thirteen women across the
world see the same terrifying vision. Their world is
about to experience ravaging destruction. All that
is now sacred will be destroyed. Each answers the call, to journey to
Egypt, and save the wisdom of the Goddess.

An imagining… or is it a remembering… of the end of matriarchy
and the emergence of global patriarchy, this book brings alive long
dead cultures from around the world and brings us closer to the lost
wisdoms that we know in our bones.

Walking with Persephone: A Journey of Midlife Descent and Renewal

Molly Remer

Midlife can be a time of great change – inner and outer. How do we journey through this…and what can we learn in the process? Molly Remer is our personal guide to the unraveling and reweaving required in midlife. She invites us to take a walk with the goddess Persephone, whose story of descent into the Underworld has much to teach us. This book is a journey of soul-rebuilding, of putting the pieces of oneself back together.

Part memoir, part poetry, part soul guide, Molly's evocative voice is in the great American tradition of sacred nature writing.

The Other Side of the River: Stories of Women, Water and the World

Eila Carrico

A deep searching into the ways we become dammed and how we recover fluidity. A journey through memory and time, personal and shared landscapes to discover the source, the flow and the deltas of women and water.

Rooted in rivers, inspired by wetlands, sources and tributaries, this book weaves its path between the banks of memory and story, from Florida to Kyoto, storm-ravaged New Orleans to London, via San Francisco and Ghana. We navigate through flood and drought to confront the place of wildness in the age of technology.

Part memoir, part manifesto, part travelogue and part love letter to myth and ecology, The Other Side of the River is an intricately woven tale of finding your flow… and your roots.

The Mistress of Longing

Wendy Havlir Cherry

The Mistress of Longing is...

An invitation to listen and trust the deep feminine that longs to be heard.

A love letter from, and for, devotion.

A prescription for a passionate and creative life.

A sacred reclamation.

A liberation of desire.

A hymn to kindness.

The voice of a modern mystic.

She of the Sea

Lucy H. Pearce

A lyrical exploration of the call of the sea and the depth of our connection to it, rooted in the author's personal experience living on the coast of the Celtic Sea, in Ireland.

This little book spans from coastal plants to the colour blue, pebbles to prayer, via shapeshifting and suicidal ideation, erosion and immersion, cold water swimming and water birth, seaweed and cyanotypes, from Japanese freedivers and Celtic sea goddesses, selkies to surfing, and mermaids to Mary.

She of the Sea is a strange and wonderful deep dive into the inner sea and the Feminine, exploring where the real and the magical, the salty and the sacred meet, within and without, and what implications this has for us as both individuals...and a species in these tumultuous times.

Dreamlike, meditative, poetic, She of the Sea is a love song. To the ocean. To becoming. To magic. To freedom.

Use of Womancraft Work

Often women contact us asking if and how they may use our work. We love seeing our work out in the world. We love you sharing our words further. And we ask that you respect our hard work by acknowledging the source of the words.

We are delighted for short quotes from our books – up to 200 words – to be shared as memes or in your own articles or books, provided they are clearly accompanied by the author's name and the book's title.

We are also very happy for the materials in our books to be shared amongst women's communities: to be studied by book groups, discussed in classes, read from in ceremony, quoted on social media… with the following provisos:

- If content from the book is shared in written or spoken form, the book's author and title must be referenced clearly.

- The only person fully qualified to teach the material from any of our titles is the author of the book itself. There are no accredited teachers of this work. Please do not make claims of this sort.

- If you are creating a course devoted to the content of one of our books, its title and author must be clearly acknowledged on all promotional material (posters, websites, social media posts).

- The book's cover may be used in promotional materials or social media posts. The cover art is copyright of the artist and has been licensed exclusively for this book. Any element of the book's cover or font may not be used in branding your own marketing materials when teaching the content of the book, or content very similar to the original book.

- No more than two double page spreads, or four single pages of any book may be photocopied as teaching materials.

We are delighted to offer a 20% discount of over five copies going to one address. You can order these on our webshop, or email us. If you require further clarification, email us at:

info@womancraftpublishing.com